Portugal Since the Revolution

Also of Interest

† *Change in the International System*, edited by Ole R. Holsti, Randolph M. Siverson, and Alexander L. George

Worker Participation and the Crisis of Liberal Democracy, Sherri DeWitt

Communism and Political Systems in Western Europe, edited by David E. Albright

The Spanish Political System: Franco's Legacy, E. Ramon Arango

Marxism in the Contemporary West, edited by Carl A. Linden and Charles Elliott

Ideology and Politics: The Socialist Party of France, George A. Codding, Jr., and William Safran

NATO--The Next Thirty Years: The Changing Political, Economic, and Military Setting, edited by Kenneth A. Myers

The Foreign Policies of the French Left, edited by Simon Serfaty

Social Structure in Italy: Crisis of a System, Sabino Acquaviva and Mario Santuccio

The Impasse of European Communism, Carl Boggs

† *Foreign Policies of Northern Europe*, edited by Bengt Sundelius

† Available in hardcover and paperback.

Westview Special Studies in West European Politics and Society

Portugal Since the Revolution:
Economic and Political Perspectives
edited by Jorge Braga de Macedo
and Simon Serfaty

This volume examines the economic and political circumstances in Portugal since the 1974 revolution. A succinct analysis of the central themes of Portuguese politics (drawing on public opinion surveys conducted in Portugal) is followed by a framework for analyzing the economic consequences of the coup. The authors then assess the influence of the IMF in Portugal and the conflict between short-run stabilization and long-range growth objectives; discuss Portugal's position within the European community with particular attention to the recent trends in labor migration, foreign investment, and trade; and point to the conflict between Portugal's political willingness to join the EEC and its awareness of potential costs--both economic and in terms of the effects of European integration on Portuguese cultural identity.

Jorge Braga de Macedo is assistant professor of economics and international affairs at Princeton University. He has taught at the Lisbon Law School, the University of Angola, the Catholic University of Portugal, and Yale University and is co-editor of the journal *Economia*. Simon Serfaty is former director of the Washington Center of Foreign Policy Research, Johns Hopkins School of Advanced International Studies, where he is now a member of the faculty.

Portugal Since the Revolution: Economic and Political Perspectives

edited by Jorge Braga de Macedo
and Simon Serfaty

Westview Press / Boulder, Colorado

Westview Special Studies in
West European Politics and Society

Copyright © 1981 by Westview Press, Inc.

Published in 1981 in the United States of America by
     Westview Press, Inc.
     5500 Central Avenue
     Boulder, Colorado 80301
     Frederick A. Praeger, Publisher

Library of Congress Catalog Card Number: 80-26632
ISBN: 0-89158-972-4

Composition for this book was provided by the editors
Printed and bound in the United States of America

Contents

Tables

Figures

Charts

Preface

The swift (less than seven hours) and bloodless (five deaths reported) collapse of the 46-year-
old Salazar-Caetano regime in Portugal on April 25,
1974, had a substantial international impact--in
Africa, in Europe, and on East-West relations. In
Africa, it accelerated the demise of the last remaining European empire as independence was promptly
granted by the new regime in Lisbon to Guinea-
Bissau, Mozambique, and Angola. This in turn had
two consequences. First, through the civil war that
erupted in Angola, great power conflicts re-entered
the arena of African politics in a manner that was
to escalate further throughout the balance of the
seventies and into the 1980's as well. To be
sure, the Soviets--and even the Cubans--had been
there before. Yet, the framework of their presence
had been drastically different: the Cold War denied
the permissibility of change anywhere, whether at
the center (Europe) or at the periphery (Africa) of
the international system. That change would take
place nonetheless was usually the outcome of
indigenous forces that were promptly embraced by
the Soviet Union, whose power continued to be
generally inadequate for overt and direct aid.
Now, however, the Soviet Union came to understand
détente as the legitimation of change at the periphery of the system, even while the status quo was
"originally" respected at the center. Endowed with
military capabilities that had been sorely lacking
in earlier years, Moscow could openly attempt to
direct the winds of change. Thus, intervention in
Angola was the first in a subsequent series of
initiatives that reflected the full scope of the
Soviet drive for global power.
In addition, the end of the Portuguese Empire
made it possible for African states to focus

specifically on the Southern African issues. In a
sense, the wars in Mozambique and in Angola had
diverted scarce African resources away from such
issues. Now, with these wars ended, Southern
Africa could become the center of African atten-
tion--Rhodesia/Zimbabwe first, then Namibia, and
last, South Africa itself. The white regime in
Pretoria understood this process all too well:
following the failure of its military efforts in
Angola, it embarked on a détente policy of its own
toward Zambia and Tanzania as it offered to help
break the deadlock in Rhodesia, whose dependence on
South Africa was all the more compelling as Salis-
bury had lost access to the Indian Ocean through
Mozambique. As it is well known, this effort did
not succeed. The United States too understood the
new diplomatic map well as, during the latter years
of the Nixon-Kissinger-Ford foreign-policy administration, it abandoned earlier speculations about
the so-called "Tar Baby option" to work toward a
settlement of these issues in such a way as to
stall further Soviet (and Cuban) advances in the
area. Pursued and increased by the Carter administration, such efforts set in motion a process that
brought about, in early 1980, a settlement that
owed a great deal to the persistence of Britain's
diplomacy and the good offices of Nigeria.

All of this, of course, the Portuguese Revolution did not cause single handedly. It did, however, act as a catalyst that brought together other
variables that had otherwise been evolving over the
years: the rise of Soviet power and global activ-
ism; the decline of U.S. power and the urge for
withdrawal; the emergence of new regional powers;
and the uncovering of the potential influence of
the underdeveloped states of the South against the
industrialized states of the North.

The consequences of the Portuguese coup were
to be no less considerable in Europe. At first, it
seemed to give a momentum to the emergence of a communist age in Southern Europe: the entry of the
Communist Party (PCP) into the Portuguese government, it was feared, would be but the first step in
a pattern that would see the Italian Communist Party
(whose main adversary, the Christian Democratic
Party, was about to be humiliated at the time of the
referendum on divorce in June 1974), the French Communist Party (whose ally in the Union of the Left
had nearly won the presidency against conservative
candidate Valery Giscard d'Estaing), and the Spanish Communist Party (whose resurgence following

Franco's impending death would show, it was widely
feared, the same general characteristics as in
Portugal). The darkest and gloomiest scenarios
were advanced, as the new "red tide" was to engulf
Yugoslavia and the North African states of Morocco
and Tunisia as well where questions of political
succession (an aging President Tito, a troubled
King Hassan, and an ailing President Bourguiba)
would be answered under the influence of powerful
regional neighbors (Russia and Algeria).

Ironically enough, rather than promoting
revolutionary advances elsewhere, the Portuguese
Revolution probably helped contain them instead.
In France, the aborted PCP-sponsored countercoup
of November 1975 precipitated a clash between the
French Socialists (PS) and their communist allies
and facilitated the PS's turn to the right--a turn
at the end of which stood the rupture of September
1977 and the electoral defeat of March 1978. In
Italy, the more extreme and offensive the PCP was,
the more moderate and conciliatory the Communist
Party (PCI) found it necessary to be. In June
1976, such "moderation" helped the PCI make substantial gains in the legislative elections that
were held that year. But the price for such moderation (displayed further when the PCI agreed to
enter the majority while staying out of the government) was enough dissatisfaction among the rank-and-
file to cause, in June 1979, the PCI's first electoral set-back since the end of World War II. As
to Spain, the political turmoil and economic dis-
array that followed the Revolution in Portugal--its
near-plunge into civil war--made the Spanish populace and political leadership weary of extremist
forces, whether from the left or from the right.
Ideologically akin to the PCI and hostile to the
PCP, Santiago Carillo's Communist Party (PCE) was
contained by the Spanish socialists on the left and
by a reasonably effective and unexpectedly stable
coalition government and constitutional monarchy.

Finally, the Portuguese coup impacted considerably on East-West relations and helped give
the word "détente" the bad connotation it carried
during the 1976 presidential campaign in the United
States. Such impact has already been mentioned:
U.S.-Soviet rivalry in Africa, and U.S. concern over
Soviet penetration in Western Europe. In the case
of the latter, the speed with which the new regime
in Lisbon opened diplomatic relations with Moscow
and several East European nations; the frequency of
missions thereafter, not to mention such troubling

developments as a Soviet request for fishing fleet
facilities at Madeira; and the creation of a
special interministerial commission to handle
relations with the Soviet Union--made the United
States (and other allies as well, including, most
particularly, West Germany) wonder over the dur-
ability and reliability of Portugal's membership
in NATO, a membership made especially important in
view of the vital need of the Azores Air Force
base, as seen during the 1973 Middle East War.
Accordingly, doubts spread as to the benefits that
might result from additional accommodation with
Moscow, and strong U.S. language objected to such
expansion of Soviet influence. Indeed, if it is
in Afghanistan that the oversimplified vision of
détente as a steady path toward East-West recon-
ciliation was seemingly buried in 1979-1980, it is
in Portugal that the initial stage of its agony
could be first perceived in 1974-75.

With the process of internal change that began
in Portugal in 1974 always wobbly and often tumul-
tuous, the Washington Center of Foreign Policy
Research thought that the time had come to appraise
the state of Portugal five years after the Revolution. In the spring of 1979, therefore, with the
generous support of the Gulbenkian Foundation, the
Washington Center sponsored a series of seminars
that reflected the Center's continuing interest in
assessing those international developments that
affect the course of U.S. foreign policy. For that
purpose, several papers were commissioned to serve
as an introduction to the seminar discussions. This
volume reproduces four of these papers, accompanied in
each case with two brief commentaries written by one
seminar participant and one specialist who could not
attend the seminar.

We wish to thank the Gulbenkian Foundation for
making this effort possible and Professor Jorge
Braga de Macedo for having agreed to be a co-
editor of the volume. We also want to thank Mr.
Mario Soares, who agreed to lead a concluding seminar
at the Center during one of his short stays in
Washington, D.C., in May 1979; and, of course, we
want to state our appreciation to all the seminar
participants who contributed immeasurably to the
making of this book.

Simon Serfaty

Johns Hopkins School of
Advanced International Studies

1
Patterns of Politics in Portugal Since the April Revolution

Thomas C. Bruneau

The purpose of this essay is to analyze the formation of a liberal democratic regime in Portugal since the 1974 military coup. To this end we will describe some aspects of the structures of politics, the dynamics of the conflicts concerning them, and the solutions proposed to resolve the Portuguese 'crisis'. There is probably little need to dwell on the continuing instability of a political system which has seen six provisional and six constitutional governments between 1974 and 1980. What is more, this condition may well continue. The potential gravity of such instability is readily understood if we recall that there are similarities between the unstable First Republic (1910-1926)-- which gave way to almost half a century of non-democratic rule--and the present system. And, as shall be seen, in the discussion of our survey data*, a substantial part of the population look back to the non-democratic Estado Novo with a certain amount of nostalgia as they compare their memories of it to the present situation of socio-economic change and hardship. Guarded optimism about the future of Portuguese democracy remains warranted. Yet, its continuation cannot be taken for granted; few anticipated the demise of the previous regime yet it collapsed suddenly and completely.

The present situation cannot be properly assessed without some prior understanding of the authoritarian regime and the revolutionary process initiated by its collapse. Since this background has been previously discussed elsewhere, it is only necessary here to review a number of the main points.[1] Political activity during the period 1928-1974 was structured within a conservative authoritarian regime created and directed by Premier Antonio de Oliveira Salazar until his

2

illness in 1968, at which point his understudy,
Marcelo Caetano, assumed control. The regime was
conservative in that it sought a return to the
stable, ordered, and class-structured society of
the 19th century, and based its legitimacy on
Catholic and corporatist doctrines. It was
authoritarian as it did not allow any serious
degree of popular participation in government. All
levels of government were controlled by those
above them, and the regime was largely autonomous
from society. Through an elaborate system of
class associations, guilds, professional associations, and institutions, including the Catholic
Church, demands were reduced through anticipation
and cooptation. Thus independent from society the

---

*The survey was supported by a Rockefeller Founda-
tion Fellowship in International Relations and administered for me by NORMA (Sociedade de Estudos
para o Desenvolvimento de Empresas). The questionnaire contains forty six main items, sixteen sub-
items, and eleven open-ended questions as well as a
series of items to define the sex, age, class, and
region of the interviewee. Dr. Mario Bacalhau and
I elaborated the questionnaire utilizing samples
from others; including, most particularly, those of
Juan J. Linz in his work on Spain. After two pre-
tests the questionnaire was administered to 2,000
individuals in a national representative sample of
Metropolitan Portugal. The universe is the whole of
the population over eighteen years of age who were
selected according to a random sampling strategy
elaborated by NORMA which gives all individuals in
the universe the same probability of selection. The
sample was stratified according to region (seven)
and the size of village or town (eleven). The work
began in the field on March 8, 1978 and was com-
pleted on April 24. The supervision was particularly rigorous in that my collaborator, Dr. Mario
Bacalhau, worked for NORMA at the time and super-
vised the fieldwork himself. Using census materials
on households and characteristics of the population
over eighteen years of age, the results are representative of Metropolitan Portugal. The survey is
discussed in some detail in Thomas Bruneau and Mario
Bacalhau, Os Portugueses e a Politica Quatro Anos
Depois do 25 de Abril (Lisbon: Editorial Meseta,
1978). Appendix I is the questionnaire and Appendix
II describes the methodology in the survey and data
analysis.

regime was not obliged to innovate or evolve, and
conflicts were not structured into the decision-
making apparatus. However, as the government
remained static, it grew increasingly less able to
adapt to.a domestic situation that was changing on
account of the African wars (from 1961) and growing economic integration with the outside world
(mainly from 1965 on). Ultimately the government
was unable to respond to the key colonial issue and
fell quickly and helplessly when those obliged to
fight the wars, i.e., the middle-ranking officers,
realized they would have to overthrow the regime to
change this, or any other important, policy.[2]
　　The legacy of this non-democratic, non-innova-
tive regime was a complete lack of structures upon
which to build a more democratic system. In over-
throwing the regime the Armed Forces Movement (MFA)
and the parties and groups that promoted and became
involved in the revolution eliminated the previously existing structures and sought to replace them
by some other complete system.[3] The question of a
new regime was so broad, so open, and the actors in
the struggle for power so diverse as to set in
motion a dynamic process that must be termed revolutionary both for its very momentum and the resulting changes in socio-economic structures. A key
actor in this process was the Portuguese Communist
Party (PCP) which had precise goals as well as
specific strategies to attain these goals. Its
prominence, jointly with that of the MFA, encouraged the emergence of other groups and parties,
many with international support, which contested
the PCP's strategy.[4] This interaction of political
forces gave rise in early 1976 to a system which is
still in process of formation but which minimizes
the alternative of the far Left and the far Right.
The importance of these alternatives is limited
further by the influence of foreign states and
organizations. Yet, even within the parameters of
the far Left and far Right there remains considerable room for change. Indeed, there is still so
much to define that the question of regime continues
at issue. While the likelihood of coups from the
Left or Right appears remote we must recall that
the First Republic collapsed more from apathy than
from the strength of the military which initially
assumed power.
　　In the light of this background, and in order
to comprehend the dynamics of the political system
that has emerged since the Constitution came into

effect in May 1976, we must define certain of its
characteristics, or axes, which condition these
dynamics and the eventual solution to the Portuguese 'crisis'. While this, the first consideration, may appear too abstract and even philosophi-
cal, it would appear that the mere scope of what
is involved in being Portuguese and appreciating
what can be expected from any political system is
central to the crisis. As the oldest continuing
imperial power the image of Portugal with colonies
(or overseas territories - o ultramar) was integral
to a national character or psyche, and was promoted
as such by the previous regime in defining Portuguese uniqueness. It is no exaggeration to state
that both the nature of the regime and the identity
of the nation itself are now in question. The
country is a mere 5 percent of its former
territory and one political system has yet to be
clearly defined. Thus, Portugal is diminished in
more ways than one: the colonies are gone, the
economy remains extremely weak, and the country can
no longer boast of dramatically distinct features.
It is simply small and poor. What is more, so much
was expected from the demise of the old regime and
was promised by various governments that it would
be difficult for any population to comprehend the
present crisis, much less one indoctrinated for so
long and never allowed to participate in politics.

While the term 'crisis' tends to be associated
with Marxist analysis it has become prevalent in
discussing the general situation in Portugal. In
our survey we attempted to ascertain whether the
population felt a crisis was at hand, the results
are unambiguous as shown below.

Many people speak of a crisis in Portuguese
society. Do you think there is such a crisis?

Yes	63%
No	5
Don't know	28
No response	4

Granted the crisis, most of our sample perceived
its most serious aspect in economic terms: lack of
jobs - 30%; the economy in general - 29%; increased
cost of living - 26%; and general social problems -
8%.

Portuguese themselves perceive this crisis
because the instability of these past five years is
compared to the stability of the old regime. Prior

to April 25, 1974 the country may not have been
progressive, just, or even promising for the
majority of the population. Emigration is one
indicator, and great masses of Portuguese voted
with their feet in seeking opportunities elsewhere.[5] A constant drain on the state budget, the
wars in Africa wore down the population, eventually
constituting a moral issue as it became clear that
a large number of people were undergoing severe
hardship and death for what was increasingly seen
as a lost cause. Yet, in the face of these overwhelmingly negative aspects, the situation was at
least predictable: it may have been bad, but it
was a known bad, and one that many could live with.
One wonders how many Portuguese living abroad
intended to return and live in their "casas Portu-
guesas". With the coup of April 25th and the subsequent revolutionary process, much was expected
and even more promised as people believed they
would enjoy all the positive aspects of the past
with the added benefits from the three D's of the
MFA: Decolonization, Democracy, and Development.
Instead, the first of these three D's resulted in
some 600,000 refugees arriving in Portugal and
making demands on the state and competing for
scarce jobs, even while Portugal lost the economic
benefits of colonies absorbing goods and providing
cheap raw materials. The second D (Democracy)
granted numerous opportunities to participate, but
it also produced extravagant promises and rhetoric
which became increasingly hollow and at odds with
the real situation. And the last D, understood as
economic development, has yet to materialize, as it
is unanimously recognized that the economic situation is parlous.[6] In general, then, the revolution
and the political system emerging from it have left
something to be desired.

There was no feasible way Portugal could have
retained the colonies, and the parties and movements attempting to gain support on this issue
have not succeeded. However, although Portugal
may not have had the power to influence events in
any case, there is disagreement about the manner in
which decolonization was effected:

    Portugal should have continued to fight   2%
    Independence should have been handled as
        it was   9
    Independence should have been granted but
        with guarantees for the Portuguese
        living there   59

A federation should have been created   6%
Don't know and no response   24

    In addition to the problems of decolonization
which can be blamed on the post-coup governments,
there were also setbacks created by the rapid
increases in petroleum prices after 1973 and the
world recession which severely limited trade options and emigration from Portugal. However, such
factors have proved to be difficult to comprehend
for a population used to order and stability, and
already disconcerted by the need to come to terms
with Portugal as a very small European country
rather than an empire spanning three continents.
To be sure, any revolution promises far more than
it can deliver, but what is unique (and particularly at issue here) is that Portugal provides a democratic system allowing for the representation of
the people's interests and feelings. Accordingly,
the political elites have good reason to be concerned if the population is discontented with the
ability of the government to govern. Such discon-
tent emerged very explicitly in our survey in all
the items concerning popular support. Thus, to the
question "Which government or regime best governed
the Country?" we gathered the following answers:

Salazar	Estado Novo	7%
Caetano		28
P. Carlos		1
V. Gonçalves	Provisional governments	8
P. Azevedo		3
M. Soares - 1st Constitutional Government		9
Don't know and no response		44

The total of 35% for the old regime contrasts to a
total of 21% for all the governments since the
revolution. The low (9%) figure for Mario Soares
came after almost two years at the head of the
First and the Second Constitutional Governments.
Those preferring the government of Marcelo Caetano
comprised 50% of all respondents whereas those
preferring M. Soares amounted to 16% only. Such
preference clearly reflects economic concerns: Of
those preferring Salazar and Caetano, 49% and 63%
respectively explained their preference in terms of
the better economic situation said to prevail then.
Only 12% of those who favored Soares reached a

similar judgment. The Soares government was
praised for its democratic aspects, but the total
here paled in comparison with the negative evaluation regarding the economy.

In more general terms the population was aware
of changes since 1974 (72% yes; 11% no; and 17% no
response). There was, however, little consensus
on the direction of change: for the better 18%;
for the worse 39%; no change 15%; and don't know
33%. Pursuing this we asked about changes in one's
personal life and found the following: for the
better 18%; for the worse 26%; no change 50%; and
no response 6%. In essence then, there is little
positive appreciation of changes since the revolution of 1974 and this is confirmed by virtually all
the questions raised in our survey. Similarly,
there is little appreciation of the governments
that have come and gone during these five years.

The political parties, as the key structures
of representation in a liberal democracy, are weak
and poorly organized in Portugal. The only party
that actually existed before the coup of 25 April
was the PCP which survived clandestinely and in
exile and, to this day, remains dogmatic and
strongly Stalinist. To be sure, the Socialist
Party (PS) antedated the coup: but founded only in
1973 in the Federal Republic of Germany, it had not
developed yet by the time of the coup. The other
main parties--the PSD (Social Democratic Party,
originally PPD) and the CDS (Social Democratic
Centre Party)--were founded after April 25.[7] A
number of implications arise from such delayed
party development. The parties are weakly structured, lacking in cadres, and still without elaborated goals, ideologies, and programs. In fact the
PS, after the PCP the most organized party, is
still headed by old liberals, or descendents of old
liberals, and is extremely unstable with regard to
middle level cadre. Except for the PCP, all the
parties are in flux internally, with numerous conflicts between their leaders, the middle level, and
whatever bases they might possess. The party
system essentially lacks a central point or fulcrum,
and during the five years that followed the coup,
each party has acted as much in reaction to the
others as for any other reason. Thus, a fulcrum
exists in the PCP which does have an organization,
ideology, and well-prepared cadre. Further, while
receiving a consistent 13% or 14% of the votes in
national elections it enjoys considerably more
support in certain regions (such as the Alentejo)

and in some sectors of the economy. Its union
organization, the CGT-IN controls some 200 plus
unions (out of a total of 500) and dominates the
whole confederation. While the PCP no longer over-
shadows the whole political arena as it did in
1975, it maintains a definite presence and controls
a substantial number of votes and structures.
Throughout these past five years, the other parties
have had to define themselves in relation to the
PCP. It is probably because it seemed to be the
only viable option to the PCP that the PS received
extensive domestic and international sanction, and
achieved its biggest electoral success in 1975 and
1976. Even in opposition to the PCP, however, the
PS as well as the PSD have defined themselves as
much more to the left than either their cadre or
their actions would suggest. The initial predominance of the PCP, then, has tended to push the
political spectrum to the left as other parties
sought to position themselves slightly to its right.
Agreement among the parties has been all the more
difficult to obtain (and consequently governmental
instability all the more exacerbated) as the PCP,
anxious to preserve its organizational integrity
and its constituency, must appear intransigeant and
faithful to its doctrine, and thus cannot allow itself to be included in coalitions.

In the three elections after 1975 (the constituent assembly elections on April 25, 1975, the
Assembly of the Republic elections on April 25,
1976, and the local elections in December 1976) the
results have reflected a predilection for political
stability. For example, the elections to the Assembly of the Republic gave 35% to the PS, 25% to the
PPD (PSD), 16% to the CDS, and 14% to the PCP.[8]
While no party received a majority, it was also
clear that most of the electorate did not support
the ten other groups or parties occupying the far
ends of the political spectrum. In reviewing the
results of these three elections, it is obvious
that--with the exception of the PS which received
national support--each party has a regional basis
of support. The implications of this for our
purposes is that these four parties can survive
and three of them in fact draw support from the PS;
something of this nature occurred in the municipal
elections in Evora in November 1978 where the PS
dropped to third place behind a PCP coalition and
the PSD.

In our survey, we asked two questions on party
preference: first, which party could govern best,

and second, which party would the respondent support if there were elections at that time. The
results are as follows:

Party	governs best	would vote for today
PCP	6 (16)%	8 (19)%
CDS	7 (19)	9 (21)
PS	17 (42)	15 (37)
PSD	7 (19)	7 (17)
UDP	1 (2)	1 (2)
other right	1 (2)	1 (2)
other left	1 (3)	1 (2)
None	11	13
Don't know	39	30
No response	10	15

If limited to those stating a preference these
results confirm past elections. However, the fact
that more than half (60% and 58%) of the respondents did not state a preference is indicative of
much potential instability. At any rate, these
results do not augur well for greater stability
within the parties or in their relationships with
one another as so much remains ill-defined.

Also related to the newness of the parties and
the one-time central role of the PCP is the fact
that all but one of the four main parties have
close foreign ties. The PS is very closely related
to the German Socialists and the Socialist International in general. The CDS is somewhat less
closely tied to the Christian Democrats in West
Germany and the international Christian Democratic
movement. And of course the PCP is very close to
Moscow but not to the "Eurocommunist" parties in
Spain and Italy. While such international links
and assistance were initially necessary, one wonders
if the Portuguese leaders do not direct too much
attention abroad while neglecting the development
of cadres and support within the country. Obviously
something can be gained by utilizing the resources
of sister parties in organizational development but
much can also be lost if the strategy encourages an
alienation from the specific situation of Portugal.

The PSD has hitherto lacked these international
links. This is not for lack of interest, but rather
because the PS has been able to effectively veto its
entry into the Socialist International and the PSD
has avoided links with other, seemingly more conservative, organizations. This absence of links
may well be an advantage for the PSD can thus
claim with some justification that it is the only

truly national party--one which is not compromised
by any foreign obligation. Quite possibly, because
of the long history of the Empire and of Portugal
itself as the oldest continuing nation state with
constant boundaries in Europe, the Portuguese have
had a high sense of their country's uniqueness.
Thus, when we asked which foreign country could
serve as a model, 59% did not respond to the
question, overwhelmingly because of an inability to
imagine another model, while 18% thought that Portugal should create its own original model. After
that the models selected ranged from the Federal
Republic of Germany and Sweden with 6%, the U.S.
(3%), France (2%), and the USSR (1%). In short,
the Portuguese do not look to any other country as
a model, and thus the strategy of attacking the
three main parties for being anti-national is
probably viable.

The question of the foreign links of the
political parties and their general reliance on
foreign assistance poses a dilemma. The country
cannot survive without continued foreign support, a
support that has been forthcoming primarily from
the Federal Republic and the United States.[9] However, it is also a very good political issue for an
"independent" party to employ and it is possible
therefore that a party could come to power with a
program pledged to diminish these very links and
supports. This is probably a false issue, and the
results of pursuing this strategy for popular support can only be negative in the long run. In the
meantime, it tends to complicate further the
political scene and to confuse the population.

Another aspect of the foreign involvement in
Portugal has been the coordinated efforts on the
part of NATO allies to encourage and assist the
Portuguese Armed Forces in assuming a larger role
within NATO. In light of the predominance of the
military in politics from the coup until early
1976, it is very important that NATO (led in this
particular instance by the United States, the
Federal Republic, and Great Britain, but with
broad support from other member states) has been
able to encourage and attract the Armed Forces into
a more restricted military role. So far this
effort has focused mainly on the Army whose brigade
assigned to the defense of the southern flank has
been equipped in part out of stocks committed to
NATO, and has been trained by the allies. To a
lesser degree, however, such interest in the de-
politicization of the Armed Forces also applies to

the Navy and the Air Force. The purpose of this strategy has been to discourage (at times quite directly) the Portuguese Armed Forces from participating directly in politics while assisting them in redefining their military role away from the colonial wars and into European and Atlantic concerns. Thus, relations between NATO allies and the Portuguese Armed Forces, together with the lamentable experience of the military when it was in direct control of the country through the MFA, has made for a non-militarized political system in Portugal.

This, however, does not imply that the military (or elements with military background) are not involved in politics. By its very nature as a new regime and one in which the armed forces are somewhat better organized than other institutions, some form of involvement is unavoidable. But the taking of positions, posturing, rumours about coups, and the like, barely continues today, and, for reasons already mentioned, it is unlikely that the armed forces will be as directly involved again in the near future as it was in the recent past--at least not as an institution. Instead, the MFA elements of the armed forces remain in power in two quite different but intricately related ways. First, and most importantly, through General Ramalho Eanes who helped defeat the attempted leftist coup of November 25, 1975: supported by the PS, PSD, and CDS in the presidential elections of June 1976, General Eanes won with some 61% of the vote (vs. his closest competitor, Major Otelo Saraiva de Carvalho, with 16%).[10] Not only does Eanes have the support of the armed forces in general, and the remnants of the MFA in particular, but his rule has also been legitimated through nationwide elections. In the Constitution promulgated in May 1976 the President is granted extensive powers to form and dissolve a government, to veto laws, and to declare war and proclaim a state of siege. Thus even though power is based in the parliament, the system is at least semi-presidential--and quite possibly more as shall be seen below. Second, the MFA remains in power to a certain degree through the continuation of the Revolutionary Council (CR) whose roles remain ambiguous. The CR was included in the Constitution pursuant to a pact between the MFA and the main parties signed in February 1976 in order to guarantee that the government would maintain a progressive orientation in line with the spirit of April 25, 1974. While the Council is supposed to

disband in 1980, its powers are presently extensive
in assisting the President (who also presides in
the CR), supervising the government, having
exclusive jurisdiction in military matters, and
judging on the constitutionality of legislation.
Not popularly-elected, the CR is a continuation of
certain sectors of the MFA and symbolizes the very
critical role they played in bringing the old
regime to an end.[11] The Portuguese political
system, then, is very much a hybrid. While government is presumably based on parties in the Assembly
of the Republic, in effect the President has extensive powers and he in turn is closely related to
the CR. The CR functions somewhat unclearly as a
balance to offset increased pressure from the
right. It plays this role less because of its
structured relationship to the system and more
because of personal relationships with the president
and contacts in the government and armed forces.

Such an indirect system--where the parties
which form the government presumably hold power but
are in effect preempted by the president whenever
necessary--may well be unavoidable in the fragile
democratic system of Portugal, faced as it is by
tremendous demands. The responses to our survey
indicate that the population supports the predominance of the presidency among the institutions
necessary for Portugal to be a democratic country:
What institution is necessary for Portugal to be
Democratic?

President of the Republic	24%
Neighborhood associations	2
Political parties	18
Organized armed forces	5
A single party	5
Other	2
Don't know	40
No response	4

The 40% who don't know is cause for concern but what
stands out is the dominance of the president of the
Republic over political parties (quite possibly due
to Eanes' demonstrated democratic goals). In fact,
in response to a question as to what individuals or
institutions really govern the country we find the
following: Which people or institutions really
govern this country now?

President of the Republic	39%
Cabinet	20
Assembly of the Republic	14
Prime Minister	26
Revolutionary Council	11
Other	1
None	2
Don't know	30
No response	3

There is therefore not only support for the President but also a widespread awareness that he does in fact govern. Together, the President and the CR receive 50% vs. 40% for the Prime Minister and the Assembly. Such a predominant role for the President--who is selected by a nationwide election--is probably necessary at these early stages of democratic formation, and is clearly supported by the population. Yet, such a situation encourages the predicament in which the political parties bicker, refuse to cooperate, and generally fail to take the exercise of power seriously. With power ultimately located elsewhere, the parties, as represented in the Assembly, can assume unrealistic positions and engage in personal attacks on each others' leaders.

This tentative nature of the political institutions also holds for the fundamental charter, the Constitution of 1976. The Constitution was written by a Constituent Assembly elected on April 25, 1975, and approved by all the deputies in Parliament except those of the CDS. Combining many elements of Western democratic experience, it is an eclectic and elaborate document in which the gains that followed the Revolution are presumably consolidated. The Constitution (which cannot be amended until 1980, and then only with a two-thirds vote of the Assembly) provides for "assuring the transition to socialism through the creation of conditions for the democratic exercise of power by the working classes" and "the development of the revolutionary process imposes, on the economic plane, the collective appropriation of the principal means of production." Formulated during a period of revolutionary fervour (when even the deliberations of the constituent assembly seemed somewhat beside the point), and by parties still defining themselves in relationships to the PCP, the Constitution is a very progressive and all-

inclusive document indeed.[12] It guarantees precisely those structural modifications which can be
called into question--and have been--when internal
and international realities are better understood.
It is, in short, a document that is extremely
advanced for a country at Portugal's level of
development in which the population, through
parties and interest groups, can express themselves.
   It is difficult to determine from the results
of our survey whether the population supports the
Constitution or not. For one, the Portuguese
appear to lack information about it (in response to
a question testing their knowledge, some 32% gave
the correct response; 51% did not know; 5% didn't
respond and 12% were in error) thereby casting
doubt on the credibility of the opinion (68% of
the population) that the Constitution can in fact
be implemented. Moreover, other responses to our
questionnaire leave open to doubt what general
support there is for the Constitution. As the many
guarantees written into the Constitution are perceived to conflict with apparently necessary
measures, there is reason to believe that there
will be a tendency to abridge the document thereby
decreasing its legitimacy. Sa Carneiro, for
instance, the leader of the PSD, has published a
long book indicating how he would replace the Constitution with one of his own making. It is on
precisely this point, revision of the Constitution,
that Left and Right are popularly defined today:
the Left (PS and PCP) is against revision, while
the Right (CDS and PSD) supports it in ever more
vigorous terms.
   One last but very important factor which
reflects the decreasing confidence in government
and erodes the legitimacy of the Constitution concerns the very substantial tasks under the direct
control of the state. It would be difficult
enough to govern in the face of socio-economic
crises, decolonization, and new political institutions even if the role of the state were more
limited. However, in Portugal the state was
traditionally central both through the corporative
system and in terms of investment policies. With
the revolution, this role increased considerably
as the banks and insurance companies were nationalized, bankrupt firms absorbed, and the techno-
crats and managers of monopolies in the previous
regime fled the country.[13] Today the state sector
has become very large with some 45% in overall
investment (vs. 18% in 1973) while public

administration has remained a holdover from the
colonial era when efficiency and competition were
not necessary considerations. As a result, the
role of the state is much greater than its ability
to enact policies, thereby leading to poor policy
implementation and general inefficiency. Ironically enough, the standard text for public administration remains Marcello Caetano's Manual de Direito
Administrativo which now is in its tenth edition.
The old administration lingers on while the many
projects and plans for the short and middle run
come and go. However impressive, the data and
aspirations found in the many governments' plans
have little to do with actual policies.[14] In the
meantime, the same administration continues as the
Ministry of Administrative Reform in the Second
Constitutional Government has had only tactical
political significance and has not reformed
anything.

The combination of these factors concerning
unstable politics and new institutions defined in
a far-reaching Constitution has created a situation
in which the question of a particular government
involves a question of the whole regime. Much was
promised in the Constitution; yet, the crises
continue. Government by the political parties has
shown severe limitations in its ability to govern
and the administration to administer. In this
context the population displays some reserve in
supporting the new political structures, and the
President is obliged to assume more power than was
intended or he personally would have desired.
These points, and their political consequences, may
best be illustrated by reviewing the governmental
instability that followed the First Constitutional
Government in July 1976.

The results of the elections to the Assembly
of the Republic gave 102 deputies to the PS, 76 to
the PSD, the CDS 41, and the PCP 40. Although in
minority, the PS decided to govern alone in a
parliamentary system requiring at least a majority
to pass legislation and remain in office. An
alliance with the PCP was eschewed both for reasons
of international considerations in a period of
Eurocommunist growth, and because the rise of the
PS to power was due to a large extent to its
opposition to the PCP during the high tide of the
revolution in 1975. Encouraged by some sister
parties (but not all) to form a coalition with the
PSD, the PS chose to go it alone in part because
of the animosity between Mario Soares and

Sa Carneiro (President of the PSD), but more
importantly in the expectation that popular support for the PSD would evaporate if it were not in
power. The government survived for some sixteen
months (a record for popularly elected governments
in Portuguese history) by generating support from
the Left on some issues, and from the Right on
others. However, as the difficulties facing the
society and the economy became more and more evident this strategy became less and less viable.
By late Summer 1977 the PCP was advocating the fall
of the government on the issue of agrarian reform.
What finally brought it down were the fundamental
issues of the General State Budget, the Plan for
1978, and the need, as spelled out by the International Monetary Fund (IMF), to have broad support
in Portugal before negotiating support of a $50
million loan which would open the way to the
"grande emprestimo" (big loan) of $750 million.
The need for this "grande emprestimo" highlighted
the serious economic situation in the country, and
in return for support the other parties demanded
participation in the government. The PS, calcu-
lating that other coalitions were unlikely if not
impossible without its participation, refused and
the government was defeated on a vote of confidence
of 100 to 159 on December 9, 1977.

The First Constitutional Government was faced
with an unenviable task, and the Portuguese were
sharply critical of its action. As already mentioned, to the question of which government
governed best, Mario Soares received only 9% of all
answers. Our survey also investigated public
reaction to the actions of the First Constitutional
Government: those who thought it governed well
amounted to only 9%, those who thought it did not
39%, and the rest either did not know (46%) or did
not respond (6%). Pursuing this question further,
we asked whether there was agreement with the
resignation of the government and found the
following:

Complete agreement	25%
Partial agreement	14
Partial disagreement	7
Total disagreement	6
Don't know or no response	48

Thus 74% of those responding agreed that the
government should have fallen.

The fall of the government was followed by a
month of intense negotiation (the IMF negotiation
was itself in abeyance) to form another government.
The same problem of achieving a coalition with
either the PCP or the PSD remained as before.
Remarkably enough, however, an agreement was concluded between the PS and the presumably rightist
CDS, which had previously opposed the Constitution.
Not a coalition as such, the resulting government
was called a PS government with the participation
of some CDS elements (three ministers and several
secretaries of state). In practice, of course,
it was a coalition and functioned as such. Again,
the PS hoped that the PSD would lose its support
while out of power. Its program was approved in
February by only the PS and CDS. However, when
Sa Carneiro consolidated his power within the party
it became evident to the CDS that further involvement in a government which of necessity had to
implement unpopular policies could reduce its power
base on the right to the benefit of the PSD. Subsequent demands by the CDS for cabinet changes were
rejected by the PS, thereby causing the disappearance of a majority in the Assembly. The President
acted rapidly and dismissed Mario Soares in July
1978.

Following these two negative experiences, and
given the continuation of the serious economic
problems, the President increased his role. For
the Third Constitutional Government he called on a
figure with little party identification, Nobre da
Costa, to form a government of other independents
with the confidence of the President. The parties
were little involved in the formation of this
government, and its program (presented in the
Assembly in September) received the support of only
the PSD and some independents. This government
remained in office slightly more than two months.

The Fourth Constitutional Government was
formed by the President in a similar manner. By
then, it was becoming increasingly clear to the
parties that the options were threefold: a party
coalition which seemed impossible; general elections; or a government initiated by the President.
Since the first two options seemed even less attractive than the third one, and as extensive consulta-
tion did take place, a government was formed under
the leadership of Carlos Alberto da Mota Pinto in
December 1978. It resigned in June in the face of
two censure motions which brought together the PS
and PCP. While the split was in part Left/Right,

there were in fact tremendous difficulties within
the government whose general popularity was
apparently quite low.

   With neither a coalition government nor one
initiated by the President viable, the latter
appointed an interim prime minister (Lurdes
Pintasilgo, in August), dissolved the Assembly of
the Republic, and prepared for mid-term Parliamentary elections. These took place on December 2,
1979, and local elections on December 16, while
regular Parliamentary elections are scheduled for
the autumn of 1980, and Presidential elections the
following year.

   The 1979 Parliamentary elections resulted in
shifts generally in accord with our survey of a
year and a half earlier. For these elections the
PSD, CDS, and the PPM (Popular Monarchists) formed
an electoral coalition--the Democratic Alliance
(AD)--while the PS ran it alone, and the PCP entered
into an electoral coalition with a movement which it
has always been close to, the MDP (Portuguese Democratic Movement), to form the United Popular Alliance (APU). The organizational weakness and ideological ambiguity of the PS, manifested in a very poor
election campaign, allowed it to slip right through
the middle of the political spectrum. This party
which had received national support in 1975 and
1976 as the main opponent to the PCP, lost everywhere (27% of the vote as compared to 35% in 1976)
but for insignificant gains in Guarda. The AD (45%
of the vote versus 41% in 1976) gained heavily in
the South and the APU (19% as compared to 14% in
1976) gained everywhere with particular success in
the North. To some, the election demonstrated a
polarization in Portuguese political life, something the PS has feared and opposed. Yet, what
seems more likely follows from our earlier comments
on the ongoing weakness and instability of the
party structures. Since the election the PS has
seen a rapid turnover in its leadership and cadres,
and is now planning a thorough reorganization. In
early 1979, something of this sort took place in
the PSD, thereby permitting the formation of the
AD.

   In light of such governmental instability a
number of proposals were made during the first half
of 1979 to change the constitution, all involving
an even more prominent role for the President. The
instability of the parliamentary system would thus
be avoided and governing would presumably become
more efficient. The President, however, after

entertaining many of these proposals made it clear
that he would not support any particular bloc of
politicians in 1980(a prerequisite to the obtention
of a majority in the Assembly that would permit the
amendment of the Constitution). Most likely
because he has emphasized time and again that he is
'President of all the Portuguese' and not of any
one particular political group, but also because
he is Chief of the General Staff, Eanes has avoided
close contact with the politicians. As a result,
while he has maintained his overall popularity he
has been in fact isolated from the politicians and
is vigorously attacked by all the parties with the
exception of the PCP.[15] For the time being at
least the alternative of a "presidential solution"
has been set aside.

The Parliamentary elections in December 1979
gave the AD 128 deputies in the 250 member Assembly
thus allowing it to form a government. In many
respects the Sixth Constitutional Government is out
of sympathy with the revolution initiated on April
25, 1974. What is more, because of the background
and role of the President of the Republic and the
CR in defending the orientation of the revolution,
the AD government is frequently in conflict with
these two institutions. This situation is likely
to continue at least until the Parliamentary elections in the autumn, and, depending on their
results and those in the 1981 Presidential elections, maybe even longer.

There are a number of conclusions that can be
drawn from this short discussion and analysis.
After fifty years of dictatorship, Portugal does
indeed have a liberal democratic system in place.
However, for historical and structural reasons, the
link between the wishes of the population and the
government has not functioned very effectively.
In the face of a certain impotence of the government, many serious economic and social problems
have not been confronted and the President has been
forced to assume a larger role in the governing of
the nation. His willingness to do this, together
with the existence and functions of the CR, have
made it less compelling for the parties to compromise in order to govern. The same might also be
said of the support of foreign states, institutions, and organizations. In providing extensive
support of all types they have probably allowed
Portuguese democracy to survive. However, such
support has also allowed a great deal of leeway to
most of the major parties who have not had to

tackle serious problems of cooperation. Thus democracy survives, but its form may well change into a
somewhat more indirect or mediated pattern in
which the parties play a diminished role. The
Portuguese case, at least up to now, shows the
limits of foreign influence. Although important
such influence has been unable to determine the
specific pattern or formula of Portuguese politics.

The population has been mildly supportive of
Portuguese democracy, but they do not identify yet
with the structures of the present regime and are
unhappy with its results. From the previous regime,
they learned not to expect much from politics, and
they are now probably coming to terms with the
unfulfilled promises of the last five years. Their
expectations should be reasonably easy to satisfy,
a point which was particularly well illustrated by
responses to two questions raised in our survey.
Asked to list the main qualities they would expect
from their leaders ("What are the main qualities
that a leader should have at this time?"), the
answers were as follows:

Honesty	23%
Firmness/courage	14
Competence	12
Dedication to people	11
Intelligence	7
A-partyness	6
Energy	5
Sincerity/coherence	5
Democracy	5
Don't know, no response	51

It is not unreasonable to expect a leader to embody
some of these qualities, and we might note that
concern with democracy is rather far down the list.
Asked what is the most important objective of the
government in the near future the Portuguese
answered:

Peace	45%
Equality	14
Order/stability	11
Socialism	10
Development	19
Liberty	4
Don't know	5
No response	1

That the country was at war for the thirteen years

before the coup overthrew the old regime precisely
for this reason, explains the overwhelming support
for peace. Otherwise, the remaining objectives
are reasonably evenly distributed, with liberty far
down the list. Again, it would seem that such
priorities, as distributed in our survey, should
not be impossible to begin to satisfy.

Combining historical considerations and international constraints, and taking into account the
survey results as well, we can probably conclude
that the liberal democratic regime will continue
even if the existing structure of power is likely
to change. To this time, the parties, in the context of a very representative parliamentary system,
have not demonstrated their ability to govern.
There is reason to fear that such failure of the
parties will decrease the legitimacy of the Constitution and the regime. While there are now no
viable anti-democratic movements or parties, the
pro-democratic forces are not very impressive either
for too often the calls for democracy are merely
transparent claims for personal and organizational
gains.

What emerges clearly from this review is the
tentativeness of the gains coming out of the revolutionary process that was initiated in 1974.
These have been real: democratic participation and
involvement, class organizations, some structural
reforms in agriculture and industry, and most
generality the ability for the people to consider
all possible (and many impossible) options. Obviously, there have also been other, negative changes
born out of processes which were, after all, brought
about through sporadic popular enthusiasm and the
encouragement of a very mixed lot of self-proclaimed
leaders. But on the whole there is much that is
positive in the revolutionary experience of Portugal, especially in comparison with what preceded it
during the Old Regime.

Presumably, these gains have been guaranteed
in the Constitution and by the parties that wrote
it. However, it is precisely in these areas (the
Constitution and the party system) that reside the
greatest structural weakness and lack of popular
support. The current President and the CR support
these gains, but another president, in a different
configuration that would give him even more power,
could easily reverse them, the opposition of the
PCP notwithstanding. Already there is a tendency
to neutralize many of these changes as Portugal is
increasingly integrated within the EEC and OECD

economies. Thus, by providing incentives for very
large firms, the Foreign Investment Code is likely
to discourage popular initiatives. Similarly, the
IMF prescription which was accepted in 1978 tends
in this direction as well. Increased integration
together with programs to attract investments
(which have so far not been forthcoming) will
undoubtedly cause increased rationalization and
consolidation of firms. It is likely that some of
the major gains in industry and agriculture will be
reversed because there is such a small political
base to retain them. The trend to deviate from the
orientation defined in the Constitution is already
clear to politically-aware constitutional experts
and my interviews with businessmen and foreign
representatives indicate that this trend is assumed
to continue.[16] It is in this context that the
terms of integration into the EEC are so important.
Portugal represents but three percent of the present Community in terms of population and one percent in terms of gross domestic product. Obviously,
the Portuguese system will be heavily affected by
entry, and while groups and individuals from the PS
to the Confederation of Portuguese Industries view
such entry as a surrogate for the lost empire this
remains to be seen. The terms will have to be
defined politically as well as economically.
Granted that the IMF prescription had essentially
economic justification, the policies of such countries as the United States and the Federal Republic
of Germany could have been in fact more supportive
of the Portuguese. Thus, whether foreign governments and organizations continue to support the
development of Portuguese democracy now that it is
threatened by the "natural" processes of trade and
investment remains to be seen.

NOTES

1. See my "Portugal: Problems and Prospects
in the Creation of a New Regime," Naval War College
Review XXIX, #1, Summer 1976, pp. 65-83.
2. The best book on the background to the
coup remains Avelino Rodrigues, et. al. O Movimento
dos Capitães e o 25 de Abril (Lisbon: Moraes, 1974).
For an account by a key element see Otelo Saraiva
de Carvalho, Alvorada em Abril (Lisbon: Livraria
Bertrand, 1977).
3. See the various contending plans and
programs defining the future of Portugal including

the following: Programa de Politica Economica e
Social of 21 February 1975; Plano de Acção Politica
of 21 June 1975; Documento-Guia Aliança Povo-MFA of
8 July 1975; Documento dos Nove of July 1975; and
Documento do COPCON also of July 1975. This is not
to mention the plans and programs of the between
twelve and fifty two political parties and groups.

4. On the interaction of the groups see my
"The Left and the Emergence of Portuguese Liberal
Democracy," in Bernard E. Brown (ed.) Eurocommunism
and Eurosocialism: The Left Confronts Modernity
(N.Y.: Cyrco Press, 1979).

5. Between 1960 and 1972 the population
declined by 3 percent due to emigration which
took about 1,500,000 people out of the country.
In 1970 the population was a little more than
8,000,000 thus the scope of the emigration can be
appreciated. On the population see Mario Bacalhau,
Portugal: Quantos Somos? (Lisbon: Terra Livre,
1977).

6. Others in this book deal with the economic
situation. I would only call attention to the
latest OECD Survey with its very gloomy description
and projection. OECD Economic Surveys: Portugal
(Paris, July 1979).

7. A useful description of the positions of
the parties in Albertino Antunes, et. al., A Opção
do Voto (Lisbon: Intervoz, 1975).

8. The election results are reproduced in
many places. See for example the results for all
the elections in Constituição da Republica Portuguesa (Lisbon: Rei dos Livros, 1977).

9. A rough estimate is the United States has
provided $175 million in PL 480 until FY 1979; $460
million in CCC until 1979; and $480 million in
various other grants and loans including balance of
payments support. The Federal Republic has provided at least 75 million marks a year in development
programs, 200 million in balance of payments support, and some part of 500 million marks for a
solidarity plan for Southern Europe. There is then
the 300 plus million units of account from the EEC
and the $750 million 'big loan' for balance of
payments. The support of other countries could be
noted as well but the above figures should be sufficient for a general idea of the level of support.
Military assistance is not included here.

10. The only book on Eanes is Paulino Gomes,
Eanes: Porquê o Poder? (Lisbon: Intervoz, 1976).

11. The Revolutionary Council is composed of
nineteen members, four of which are members by

virtue of their posts. Others are elected within
their arms. Lieutenant Colonel Ernesto Melo
Antunes remains a key figure in the CR.
     12. There are many books dissecting and
analyzing the constitution. Probably the most
complete is the 856 page tome by Reinaldo Caldeira
and Maria do Ceu Silva, Constituição Politica da
Republica Portuguesa, 1976 (Lisbon: Livraria
Bertrand, 1976).
     13. For a listing and discussion of the firms
under various forms of state, ownership and control
see M. Belmira Martins and J. Chaves Rosa, O Grupo
Estado: Analise e Listagem Completa das Sociedades
do Sector Publico Empresarial (Lisbon: Edições
Jornal Expresso, 1979).
     14. See for instance the Plano para 1977, the
multi-volume Plano de Médio Prazo, and the Projecto
de Plano para 1978.
     15. On Eanes' popularity see Mario Bacalhau,
Eanes: A Solução? (Lisbon: Heptagono, 1979).
     16. The constitutional aspects are dealt with
by Marcelo Rebelo de Sousa, Direito Constitucional
(Braga: Livraria Cruz, 1979), pp. 336-41. My
interviews on this topic were conducted in October
1978 and September 1979.

COMMENT

Some Comparative Thoughts on the Transition to Democracy in Portugal and Spain

Juan J. Linz

     The analysis by Thomas Bruneau on the problems
associated with the consolidation of democracy in
Portugal has stimulated me to ask some questions
about different routes followed by Portugal and
Spain in the process of dismanteling two long-lived
authoritarian regimes and attempting to consolidate
two new democracies. The two countries of the Iberian peninsula share many characteristics and their
political history in the last two centuries presents
parallelisms but also some significant differences.[1]
Today perhaps more than in the past, their social
and economic structures differ considerably. But
both have undertaken in the seventies the difficult
task to establish new democratic institutions. They
have done so by very different processes. In one
case a break with the past--ruptura--by golpe that
at some point appeared as a revolution, and in the
other by what is known in the Spanish political language as reforma pactada or ruptura pactada. Those
two terms refer, from different perspectives and
with different value connotations, to a process of
negotiation between the legitimate heirs of the
Franco authority and the democratic opposition. Reform by agreement from the perspective of the Establishment and breakthrough by agreement from the
perspective of the opposition.
     The political process subsequent to the in-
storation of democracy differed decisively as a result of that initial step golpe versus reform. The
role of different actors in the process could not be
more different. And as consequence, the party system, the position of the trade unions, the role of
the armed forces, the relationship between the new
leadership and the men of the past, etc., would also
be different. The enactment of the Constitution,
the institutions created in that fundamental law,

that has very important consequences for the political process, would also be quite distinct and pose
different problems for the future. One fundamental
difference between Portugal and Spain is that the
former is a republic with strong presidentialist
components and the latter a parliamentary constitutional monarchy. Some of the distinctive problems
of both countries are derived from these institutional characteristics, independently of the nature
of their respective party systems and the strength
of political parties. A decisive factor in the
process of consolidation of democracy in Portugal
is the fact that it is the oldest, and most internally homogenous in terms of language and culture,
nation state of Western Europe, while Spain after a
period of unitary and centralized government is
forced to recognize politically its multilingual
and multinational character in a constitution that
for the first time speaks of nationalities in addition to a Spanish nation.[2] Perhaps this last of
the differences we have noted is the most decisive
in explaining some of the contrasts between the two
new democracies in the process of consolidation.
It should be noted that in our counterposition we
have fundamentally referred to political processes,
institutions, and problems, but it would be a mistake to ignore some of the implications of the different levels of economic development of the two
societies. The lower level of economic development, to some extent, has complicated the Portuguese process but to another extent, made it perhaps easier to face the difficult times of the late
70's and 80's in the world economic context.
   A fully adequate analysis of the implications
of the paths followed by Portugal and Spain in
their exit from their respective authoritarian
regimes would exceed the limit of this comment.
Let us emphasize that each of them has its advantages and costs that are not easy to define and
whose perception in part depends on the political
and ideological position of the observer. The reforma pactada of Prime Minister Suarez had the advantage of what Giuseppe DiPalma has called backward
legitimation,[3] since it meant that those who were
loyal without strong ideological commitments to the
existing authorities of the Franco regime could not
question the new democratic institutions that had
been legally enacted according to the rules set
down by Franco, even though the process had much of
what the Germans in describing the transition from
Weimar to Hitler called a legal revolution. The

legal continuity, although the basis of legitimation changed totally and ran counter the spirit of
the Franco Fundamental Laws, made it easy for the
armed forces and the bureaucracy to accept the new
order and serve it without questioning it.   It
assured the relatively peaceful and smooth transition in a country where the memory of a Civil War
that had ended only 37 years earlier was still a-
live.   It has meant that those who fought on opposite sides can live together in the same society
and that those who served the Franco regime to the
extent they are willing to accept the new democratic
institutions enjoy all the rights of citizenship.
It has meant that a large segment of the elite of
the old regime can participate in public life and
in the electoral process, in contrast to Portugal
where a significant number of it was forced to go
into exile, lost its position in the administration,
and was not allowed to organize its own political
parties.   There is, however, a debit to that apparently successful path to democracy without dis-
continuity.   It certainly could not provoke the
same kind of feeling of change, of exultation in
their triumph, of the opposition, nor did it allow
the kind of semi-revolutionary and sometimes revolutionary changes in the social structure and the
power relations in the society that took place in
Portugal under the provisional governments before
the enactment of the constitution and the consolidation in power of the moderates.   The lack of revolutionary changes in the composition of the elites,
in the allocation of social power, in some basic
policies like agrarian reform and socialization of
capitalist enterprises, has made the transition to
democracy disappointing for those who value social
change as much or more than democratic political
institutions.   The drop in electoral participation
from 1977 to 1980, the widespread feeling of disen-
chantment, the sometimes ambiguous reactions of the
left opposition, the feeling often expressed that
nothing has changed and that Spain is not yet a
democracy, are some of the costs of the reforma-
ruptura pactada.   This certainly contrasts with the
enthusiasm and hopes generated by the "revolution
of the flowers".   Perhaps under more favorably economic circumstances and with greater effectiveness
of governments the Portuguese process could have led
to a stronger identification of the population,
particularly the working classes, with a new regime
than the path followed in Spain.   However, if we
turn to the survey data collected by Norma in

Portugal and DATA in Spain in 1978, our expectations, perhaps for the reasons just pointed out, are
not confirmed.[5] This is not the place to argue if
a true _ruptura_ like the Portuguese was possible in
Spain and who is to blame for its not having been
undertaken. One factor was certainly totally different in Portugal and in Spain. The Portuguese
armed forces had undergone a process of radicaliza-
tion as a result of the colonial wars that expressed
itself in the "Revolution of the Captains" and the
political role of the Movimento das Forcas Armadas
(MFA), while in Spain, even though there were some
weak beginnings of a similar movement in the army,
the institutional cohesion of the armed forces was
never in doubt and there was no prospect that a
segment of the army would have forced a true _rup-
tura_ upon the heirs of Franco. For a variety of
circumstances, Santiago Carrillo recognized at the
first congress of the communist party in freedom
that the _ruptura_ was probably impossible.[4] In
Spain the regime was certainly in crisis, opposition was mounting, the terrorist activities of the
ETA in the Basque Country posed a serious problem,
but ultimately there was no unsolvable problem like
the colonial wars were for the Caetano regime. In
Spain there was no reason for the armed forces to
move to the "liberation by golpe" and without their
support or at least total neutrality the _ruptura_
model was not viable, while fortunately the _reforma_
became _reforma pactada_ and ultimately, _ruptura
pactada_. There remains the interesting question
why after the incapacity and the death of Salazar,
Caetano was not able to undertake a similar process
to the Spanish, particularly considering that the
country was less intensely politicized and that
probably the conservative and highly populated
north of Portugal would have given electoral support to a center right party as the carrier of such
a process. Perhaps the failure of Caetanismo in
Portugal made it even clearer to King Juan Carlos
that the slow process of half hearted reform
initiated by Arias and the most progressive members
of his cabinet was doomed and that a new and different approach was needed. In a sense, the events
in Portugal between April 1974 and the death of
Franco in November 1975, made the Spanish elite
more conscientious of the risk of delaying unduly
the dismantling of the old regime and of the need
to take steps that would allow what DiPalma calls
forward legitimation, by calling for free elections
and legalizing the communist party.

In this context, one cannot overestimate the importance of the King as an arbitrator in the situation, as the focus of loyalty for the armed forces, as a symbol of continuity for some and hope for others, and as a decisive actor without running the risks of holding executive power. The question might be asked why the President of the Portuguese republic could not or did not want to play such a role when the failure of Caetano in finding political solutions became apparent. One might ask the same question about Spinola as a provisional president.

One important difference of far reaching implications between liberation by golpe and democratization by a law for political reform (let us note it is not of political reform), is the very different role played by the army. The Portuguese armed forces first as a movement and later as an institution, as MFA and as FAP (Forcas Armadas Portugueses) were a visible political actor, compared to the "invisible", although not unimportant role of the Spanish army in the transition. A difference of decisive significance. The leading actors in the Spanish process were the King and civilian politicians, while in Portugal some of the key persons were military officers who only reluctantly started incorporating civilian politicians, and forced them to sign the pact between the parties and the armed forces before allowing them to make a Constitution.

The persistence of the Council of the Revolution as an institution with veto powers potentially can limit the full sovereignty of the parliament accountable to the electorate and as shown in Bruneau's chapter leads to a complex triangle of relations between parliament, the President, and the Council that now is up to debate in the reform of the Constitution. It could be argued that the armed forces in Spain as a poder factico, to use the Spanish terminology (power of fact or 'real' power, playing with the latin words in their translation) and the relationship between them and the King are the functional equivalent. Such an analysis is certainly a temptation for the political scientist in the behavioral tradition, but ignores some fundamental differences between de facto and legal power. De facto interventions are only likely in extreme situations, can be muted or invisible and thereby create less conflict in the body politic, are less divisive within the armed forces and do not commit the actors to public

TABLE 1.1
Opinions about the aspects in which there has been change toward better or worse or no change in Portugal and Spain (1978).

Aspects of national life	For better	No change	For worse	d.k.	Difference better-worse
Freedom					
Portugal	51	4	21	24	+30
Spain	67	11	17	5	+50
Wages					
Portugal	44	8	25	23	+19
Spain	22	25	47	6	-25
Politics					
Portugal	33	7	26	34	+7
Spain	57	14	23	7	+34
Development/Progress					
Portugal	16	23	28	34	-12
Economic Development					
Spain	25	33	34	7	- 9
Economy					
Production					
Portugal	3	6	61	30	-58
Spain	5	9	48	38	-43
Labor Relations					
Portugal	12	10	50	28	-38
Labor Conflicts					
Spain	32	42	19	7	+13

Education					
Portugal	11	17	40	32	-29
Spain	32	42	19	7	+13
Morality					
Portugal	10	15	47	28	-37
Spain	29	23	44	5	-15
Regional Autonomies					
Spain	63	14	15	8	+48
The "living together" (convivencia) of Spaniards	41	30	23	6	+18

Source: Portugal, IFOP, op. cit., p. 112. Spain, Survey by DATA, July 1978.

stances, and therefore quite different in their consequences. It seems unlikely that if the armed
forces would have had in the Spanish Constitution
the legal positions they occupy in Portugal, their
role in the negotiation of the autonomy statutes
would not have made the consociational policies
pursued by Suarez and Garaicotxea more difficult or
impossible.

One of the paradoxes of the recent past of the
two countries is that while Portugal experienced a
political and to a large extent a social revolution,
particularly in some parts of the country, and at
some point the threat of civil war loomed large,
the number of victims of political violence has
probably been and is likely to continue being smaller than in Spain. In the first phases of the
transition this difference might be attributed to
the repression exercised by the Spanish authorities
against the threats of ruptura, but ultimately
mostly to the actions of the terrorists of the ETA
and the climate created by its supporters in the
Basque country. There is the temptation to attri-
bute the different rates of violence to differences
in the national character, but it could be argued
that it has been one of the costs of the reforma
model with its slow and halting process of change,
the desilusion of radical groups and opportunities
for right wing extremists organizations, that could
not and were not supressed legally early. We obviously do not know and cannot estimate how many
victims would have resulted from a more revolutionary process in a more complex and divided, advanced
industrial and organized society. A process that,
in a country in which a period of prosperity and
rapid upward mobility had raised expectations,
would have made the type of changes that took place
in Portugal much more threatening and frustrating
for a much larger upper and middle class.

The interesting survey data presented by
Bruneau and collected by him in collaboration with
Bacalhao in part contradict the preceding analysis
when compared with those of DATA for Spain.[5] There
are clear indications that the memory of the Salazar, but above all the Caetano period in Portugal,
are more positive than those of the Franco period,
and that this positive evaluation of the past regime
is more widespread even among the supporters of the
democratic parties, including the socialists, than
in Spain. The ease with which the old regime had
fallen, the achievement of peace with decolonization, the relatively modest social and economic

TABLE 1.2
Opinions about the regime that governed the country best (Portugal) and about the
actions of Franco (Spain) by party preference.

	Total	Extreme Left	PCP PCE	PS PSOE	PSD	UCD	CDS	AP	Other Right	None	d.k. n.a.
PORTUGAL Regime that governed best:											
Salazar	7	--	3	4	7		10		39	15	7
Caetano	28	18	18	22	55		69		54	31	19
	(6091)	(120)	(480)	(936)	(450)		(532)		(41)	(769)	(2762)
SPAIN Opinion about Franco:											
Approve totally	10	3	1	3		15		43	51	6	8
Acted fairly well	19	3	2	7		34		46	25	14	23
	(5898)	(99)	(599)	(1842)		(1573)		(381)	(65)	(324)	(648)

Source: Portugal: IFOP, op. cit. p. 39. Spain: Survey by DATA, July 1978.

33

advances before the revolution would have led us to
expect a more positive response to the post 1974
government. Undoubtedly, some of the factors mentioned by Bruneau on the negative side seem to weigh
heavier, but probably the higher levels of politi-
zation in Spain in the 30's, the memories of the
Civil War and its aftermath, account for the
stronger rejection of Franco by large parts of
population. In addition the change in outlook of
the new generations, already initiated under Franco,
explains the less positive response of the social
classes logically more inclined toward the regime.
The absence of certain forms of economic and social
dislocation due to the reform and the electoral
success of the center right coalition, the UCD,
probably also has facilitated the desidentification
from the past. On the negative side, we might note
that opinions about the past in Spain are more
polarized and that therefore any involution toward
authoritarian solutions of a crisis would be more
conflictual and bloody in Spain than in Portugal.
In Spain, it would encounter the resistance not
only of the working class left, particularly the
communist party (as in Portugal), but also the
unanimous opposition of the Basque country and a
nearly unanimous one in Catalonia.

The difference between the revolutionary ruptura and the reforma pactada has also had long
range consequences for the distribution of power in
the society. In Portugal, it allowed the communist
party to take over the existing trade union organization through the control of the Intersindical,
while in Spain it led to the emergence of a politically divided trade union movement where those
opposed to the communist hegemony could from the
beginning create their own organizations, mainly
the socialist Union General de Trabajadores, UGT.
The Portuguese developments in 1974 allowed the
communist party to occupy not only positions of
political power south of Lisbon, but also of social
power in a way that has no parallel in Spain. The
opportunity for a revolutionary strategy seized
after some initial hesitation by the Portuguese
communists, has assured them the powerful position
described by Bruneau, but also their political
isolation and greater ilegitimacy within the new
democracy. Their Spanish comrades independently of
their Euro-communist ideological positions before
legalization, could not experience the temptation
of striving for hegemony. They were forced by the
circumstances to proclaim even more loudly their

moderation and strive for legitimation within the
new democratic order by recognizing, almost in
exchange for legalization, the monarchy, the flag,
and the status of the armed forces, and participate
in the economic and political equilibration efforts
of the Moncloa pacts and the making of the compromise Constitution. In the process they have gained
probably a much greater legitimacy, neutralized
potentially intense hostility, and avoided isolation by the other parties. Their important presence
in local government, thanks to the municipal pact
with the socialist PSOE, has been for them the
positive side of that policy. The very different
position of the two communist parties in the future
will not be only a question of their ideological
stances, but of the very different role they played,
partly due to the circumstances, in the initial
period of institutionalization of the two
democracies.

Political sociologists and even political
scientists have become increasingly neglectful of
the comparison of political institutions and the
analysis of their implications for the functioning
of political systems. However, the extensive
reference by Bruneau to the role of the presidency
in Portugal, the public opinion data showing the
importance attached to the institution, the speculations on the role of President Eanes and his
possible successor should help to correct that neglect. Portugal's Constitution places it among the
countries that Werner Kaltefleiter[6] has characterized as having bipolar executives, a list that
includes the Weimar Republic, Finland, and the
French Fifth Republic, political systems in which
parliament and the government it produces and supports are potentially confronted with a President
with considerable powers and with the legitimacy
(at least in three countries) derived from direct
popular election and considerable autonomy from the
political parties, although they concurred in the
process of his nomination and election. The complex relationship between the President and the
parliament, between a man and both parties and
politicians, as Kaltefleiter has shown, varies considerably depending on the party system and the
capacity and willingness of the party leaders to
defend their arena of parliamentary politics, produce stable party governments, and make presidential
encroachments unlikely or difficult. In the case of
Portugal, this process is further complicated by
the relationship between a military president and

the armed forces and the special place they occupy in the Constitution through their presence in the Council of the Revolution.

As Kaltefleiter has shown, the dynamics of the bipolar executive depend fundamentally on the degree to which the party system is structured and effective in producing majority support in parliament for a Prime Minister.[7] The Portuguese experience confirms something that the social democratic leaders Breitscheid and Hilferding had already known. As Hilferding wrote, "There can be no doubt when the parliament fails in its fundamental and most important function, the forming of the government, the power of the Reichs-president is increased at the cost and by fault of the parliament, and that the President has to carry out functions which the Reichstag fails to perform."[8] The appointments of the Nobre da Costa, Mota Pinto, and Pinta Silgo governments are evidence of the play of these reserve powers of the President, the abdication of the parties from their responsibility and, to some extent, a loss of democratic authenticity. As Rainer Lepsius[9] has shown for Weimar, parliament could fall back on a passive role of toleration and revert to its veto powers without being forced to formulate a political course of action of its own. This could be seen as functional given the fragmented party structure. It could, however, also prolong the party structure disfunctional for a parliamentary democracy. Faced with difficult and painful decisions, the socialist party in Portugal could attempt with only a plurality its claim to hegemony and to avoid distasteful coalitions because the constitutional provisions provided a temporary way out. In Kaltefleiter's view, the bipolar executive model can only work well when the President is also the leader of the party or has considerable influence on a party in a well structured and not fragmented and stalemated party system. In view of the dynamics of the Portuguese party system and the constraints or tendency toward a non-party military man in the presidency, the Constitution with a bipolar executive is unlikely to change this situation.

In the Spanish Constitutional Monarchy, parliament is formally the only legitimate democratic source of power and the position of the larger parties indispensable in the formation of governments is reinforced by Article 113 inspired in Article 67 of the Bonn Fundamental Law that requires for the introduction of a censure motion the nomination

of the candidate to the Prime Ministership, making
it difficult for negative coalition to overthrow
a cabinet.[10] It is difficult to say if the relative stability of Spanish governments since the
first election under the same Prime Minister and
with only minor adjustments within a monocolore
cabinet has been reinforced by this provision or has
been the result of party alignments, ultimately, the
possibility of the plurality of the UCD to obtain
the support of a minority on the right and on occasion of the regional moderate parties. A situation that was quite different in the case of Mario
Soares, despite the fact that the parliamentary
position of the Portuguese socialist party was
stronger than that of the UCD.[11] The absence of
minor parties that could swing their support to him
and the different relation that the communist had
to the socialists in Portugal, compared to Alianza
Popular in relation to the UCD, might be the
explanation.

It could be argued that should the Spanish
multi-party system not work, should a serious crisis
occur within the strongest party in parliament, or
should the election produce the need for a coalition
between the UCD and the PSOE, the King might be
tempted to use his influence in the selection of
the Prime Minister and the internal politics of
parties, with some of the consequences we have seen
and might see in the future in Portugal. In fact,
such a prospect might be seen as, or more, destabil-
izing of the new democracy since it would put the
King and a new, and not that strongly legitimate,
monarchy into discussion. Certainly that temptation exists, but a monarch who does not face the
problem of re-election might be less tempted than
a President, particularly a popularly elected
President, to play an independent political role [12]
when frustrated by the bickering of party leaders.

One aspect of political systems we have little
information about is the degree of legitimacy
achieved by the Constitution in both countries.
The Portuguese, while in some respects a compromise,
reflects in many of its articles a particular
political ideological and social constellation.
It is a Constitution of the left, while the Spanish
has been the result of the consenso, the constant
bargaining between parties and voted by all major
parties except the Basque nationalists and a
minority of the deputies of Alianza Popular. This
broad consensus, that was not achieved in Portugal
where the Centro Democratico Social voted against

the Constitution, has been paid for by the ambiguity
of many of its provisions and the need for a large
number of controversial additional organic laws.
The Spanish Constitution offers to all major parties the possibility to govern within its framework,
while the Portuguese presents serious obstacles
for a center right or rightist policy and, therefore, has raised question of constitutional reform.
The fact that so soon after enactment this should
be a serious issue in Portugal undoubtedly contrib-
utes to divide the political elite, to arouse some
sectors of public opinion, and prevents the country
from overcoming the constitution-making phase to
turn to more pressing economic and social issues.
In Spain much depends on the continued support for
the constitutional consensus and the willingness to
raise constitutional issues of the parties; only
the development of the regional autonomies is likely to make the Spanish 1978 Constitution
controversial.

In Spain the populace probably has only a
limited understanding of the significance of the
Constitution, but the fact that 68 percent of the
voters participated in the referendum and that 88
percent of those voting approved it (except in the
three Basque provinces where the appeal for abstention by the PNV was followed by a large number of
voters with only 45.5 percent voting and of them
68.8 percent voting yes), has given to the basic law
considerable democratic legitimacy. It would be
hard to say that the Portuguese Constitution has an
equally solid basis of support.

The abstention and the negative votes on the
Constitutional Referendum in the Basque country
point, (with only 31.1 percent of the electorate
supporting the Constitution) however, to one basic
difference between Spanish and Portuguese democracy. Portugal, whatever disagreements might
exist among Portuguese is for all of them a nation
state, while in Spain significant minorities have
an ambivalent attitude toward that nation state and
a small but intense minority in the Basque country
supports independence. This is probably the most
significant difference between the two countries
and, if we add to it the terrorist activities of
the ETA, the greatest danger for the new Spanish
democracy.

While Portugal combined the transition to
democracy with considerable social and economic
change that to some extent deserves the name of
the revolution, the transition in Spain was combined

with a deep questioning of the unitary centralist
state and the emergence of a new multilingual and
multinational policy, with considerable devolution
both to nationalist and regional peripheries. In
both cases the accumulation of political change
toward a democracy with other basic and to some
extent threatening changes, has undoubtedly complicated the process of consolidation of democratic
institutions. In the measure that the fundamental
change in power relations between center and periphery in Spain satisfies the aspirations of the
periphery, until now it would seem that the majority of Spaniards has accepted this change. In the
long run, it might be a greater change than the
social economic changes of the Portuguese revolution and a more permanent source of tensions. To
the extent that the Basque nationalists would not
accept the Constitution and the Autonomy Statutes
derived from it as a more or less permanent settlement, the result might be disappointing. To the
extent that in Portugal the social economic changes
have coincided with the world economic crisis, disrupted the process of capitalist development initiated under Caetano, combined with the accumulated
structural problems and compounded by decoloniali-
zation, these important changes one might have
thought would provide the regime with what Otto
Kirchheimer[13] would have called constituent policies
have not had a legitimizing impact. The Norma survey data at least make it questionable.

There is in Portugal a widespread feeling of
crisis even when it is not clear to what aspect the
respondents were referring when they answered in
the affirmative the question, Is there a crisis in
Portuguese society? We do not know to what extent
the response refers to the economic crisis, to a
deeper social crisis, or a political crisis. The
fact that those supporting the parties of the left,
particularly the communists, should frequently say
yes might indicate that the economic factor must
weigh heavily, but it could also be a reflection of
the disappointment with an arrested revolution. The
data we have for Spain for the same year 1978 show
also a sense of crisis particularly on account of
the economic situation, but much less so about the
political situation. An absolute majority of the
respondents in Spain feel that "while there still
remained many problems to be solved in general we
cannot complain" when it came to the political situation. The figures for the economic situation were
almost the reverse. It is particularly interesting

TABLE 1.3
Opinions about the existence of a crisis in Portuguese society and about the Spanish political and economic situation (1978) by party preference.

	Total	Extreme Left	PCP PCE	PS PSOE	PSD	UCD	CDS	AP	Other Right	None	d.k. n.a.
PORTUGAL There is a crisis in Portuguese society:											
Yes		75	79	65	71		66		63		
No		8	5	11	12		1		–		
d.k.		18	11	22	15		31		34		
n.a.		5	5	2	2		2		3		
SPAIN The political situation is "everyday more serious"...	39	39	48	37		32		54	88	49	39
there remains problems..	57	57	49	60		63		43	9	43	49
n.a.	5	3	3	3		5		3	4	8	12

The economic situation is:									
"everyday more serious"...	54	78	63	55	43	59	83	62	51
"there remain problems"..	44	19	36	44	56	41	17	36	43
n.a.	2	3	1	1	1	1		2	7
	(5898)	(99)	(599)	(1842)	(1573)	(381)	(524)	(648)	

Source: Portugal: IFOP, op. cit., p. 120. Spain: Survey by DATA, July 1978. Answers to the question: "If a friend from abroad would ask you a judgement about the present Spanish political (economic) situation, what would you say (of these two alternatives). The situation is every day more serious and one cannot go on like that. There are still many problems to be solved, but in general we cannot complain."

to compare the responses of the supporters of the
government party in both countries. In Portugal 65
percent of the supporters of the socialist party
felt that there was a crisis while in Spain 45 percent of the UCD supporters perceived the economic
situation as getting everyday more serious and one
cannot go on like that, and 32 percent say the same
thing about the political situation. Even taking
the most negative response in Spain the level was
considerably below the Portuguese, only the extreme
right in both political and economic matters and the
extreme left in judging the economic situation
reached a level of criticism comparable to the Portuguese left of the socialists. Obviously, this
comparison based on Table 1.3 has to be considered
indicative since the questions asked in the two
countries were far from exactly comparable.

There are many aspects in which the foreign
policy context, the linkages between parties and
their homologous parties in Europe, have contributed
in very similar ways to the political development
in the last years in both countries. There are,
however, some differences: Portugal in spite of
the pressures on the left in the direction of the
neutralist position, due to its greater economic
dependency on Western Europe and the scare produced
by the communist ambition of hegemony, finds itself
closer to the EEC countries than Spain. The fact
that Portugal was already before the revolution a
member of NATO and has continued that tie throughout the whole transition period in spite of all the
tensions, has eliminated from the political debate
an issue that if mismanaged could become quite dis-
ruptive in Spain. Portuguese migration overseas
including to the United States together with the
smallness and weakness of the country, makes for an
easier integration into the western community of
nations.

It would have been tempting to list in a single table the many factors we have been discussing
briefly, contrasting the two countries, and even
more tempting to indicate with a plus or a minus
sign and in a few cases an equal sign the positive
and negative, indifferent or difficult to evaluate
contribution those factors made to the stability
and prospects of democracy in the two Iberian countries. Limitations of space and even more, caution, prevent us from doing so. In addition not all
readers would agree with the evaluation attributed
to each factor, particularly if we consider that
different readers would like to see quite different

democracies developed and factors positive to one
type of democracy would be negative for another;
therefore, the signs to be attributed to each
factor might very well be quite different for different readers. We can only invite the readers to
make their own try on this difficult exercise.

The comparison we have made might strike as
neglecting the economic and social structural factors unduly. Certainly, in a longer and different
essay it would have been interesting to analyze
more thoroughly the important differences in this
respect between the two countries and their potential political implications. In doing so, we
would have had to go much more deeply into a comparison of the relationship between the class structure and parties, between social position and
political behavior and attitudes. However, to do
so would require further secondary analysis of
electoral data and above all of available public
opinion surveys, and preferably a comparative
study of public opinion toward the process of
change, the past and the future, and the institutions and social forces in the two new democracies.
To design such comparative study and an adequate
survey to provide it with data would be an exciting
but difficult task. A few tables we have included
in this essay based on work done by Bruneau and
Bacalhau in Portugal and DATA in Spain should serve
to point out the fruitfulness of such an approach.

NOTES

1. Stanley G. Payne, "Spain and Portugal", in
Raymond Grew, ed. Crises of Political Development
in Europe and the United States, Princeton, Princeton University Press, 1978, pp. 197-218.
    2. Herminio Martins, "Portugal", in Margaret
S. Archer and Salvador Weidenfeld and Nicolson,
1971. For the contrast with Spain see Juan J. Linz
"Early State Building and Late Peripheral Nation-
alisms against the State", in S. N. Eisenstadt and
S. Rokkan eds. Building States and Nations, Beverly
Hills: Sage, 1973, pp. 32-116.
    Juan J. Linz, "The Basques in Spain: Na-
tionalism and Political Conflict in a New Democracy",
in Philip Davison and Leon Gordenker eds. Nation-
ality Conflict, New York: Praeger, 1980 (forthcoming).
    3. Giuseppe Di Palma, "Left, Right, Left,
Right - or Center? On the Legitimation of Parties

44

and Coalitions in Southern Europe", Conference on Mediterranean Europe, IPSA, Athens, May 1978.

4. The Communist interpretation can be found in this revealing text: "The radical ruptura carried out in one strocke, with the instauration of a provisional government, as the Communist party and the Junta Democratica proposed, was not possible for various factors, among which one can highlight the reformist orientation taken by some forces of the opposition and of those that emerged of the francotte regime itself, as well as the international pressure, mainly European and American, fearful of the hegemony of the working class and the forces of the left. These factors contributed in that the mass movement, in spite of its broadness and importance, would not achieve the necessary force to determine a radical rupturista policy. That situation obliged the PCE to nuance its rupturista theses in the ruptura pactada. And, in fact, the process of change has been developing as such a ruptura pactada, even though that pact is purely tacit, after the displacement by the mass struggle of the reactionary and inmobilist government of Arias Navarro." Thesis I of the 15 theses presented by the Central Committee for discussion at the IX Congress of the PCE on April 5-9, 1978, sent to all members of the party, Mundo Obrero, Especial IX Congreso (II), p. 1.

5. Instituto de Estudos de Desenvolvimento, Sondagem a opiniao publica dirigido por Thomas Bruneau y Mario Bacalhau, Os Portugueses e a politica. Quatro anos depois do 25 de abril, Lisboa: Editorial Meseta, 1978, survey of 1991 interviews carried out between March 8 and April 24 in continental Portugal (the weighted sample was 6091).

6. Werner Kaltefleiter, Die Funktionen des Staatsoberhauptes in der parlamentarischen Demokratie, Cologne; Westdeutscher Verlag, 1979, chapter 4, pp. 129-97.

7. See graph on p. 187 of Kaltefleiter, op. cit.

8. Quoted by Kaltefleiter, op. cit. pp. 162-63 from an article in Die Gesellschaft. Internationale Revue fur Sozialismus und Politik, 7, 1, 1930, p. 389.

9. Rainer Lepsius, "From Fragmented Party Democracy to Government by Emergency Decree and National Socialist Takeover: Germany", in J.J. Linz and A. Stepan, eds. The Breakdown of Democratic Regimes, Europe, Baltimore: Johns Hopkins University Press, 1978, pp. 34-79, see pp. 46-50.

10. For a commentary on the Constitution see Oscar Alzaga, Comentario sistematico a la Constitucion espanola de 1978, Madrid: Ediciones del Foro, 1978.

11. Portugal has had four prime ministers and five cabinets since the approval of the Constitution. Spain since the first free election in 1977 (to May 1980) has had four cabinets under prime minister Suarez.

12. Antonio Bar Cendon "La 'Monarquia Parlamentaria' como forma politica del Estado Espanol segun la Constitucion de 1978", in Manuel Ramirez ed. Estudios sobre la Constitucion Espanola de 1978, Portico, Zaragoza, pp. 193-215.

13. Otto Kirchheimer, "Confining Conditions and Revolutionary Breakthroughs", American Political Science Review, 59, 1965, 964-74.

COMMENT

Eusebio Mujal-Leon

While addressing the question of what the perspectives are for the consolidation of democracy
in Portugal, Professor Bruneau's essay points to the
tenuous character of the gains made in that country
since the April 1974 revolution, and the ambiguities
and contradictions of the present situation. With
the Portuguese people and political elite unable to
define clearly the nature of the society in which
they wish to live, Professor Bruneau examines the
resulting clash between alternative definitions of,
and projects for, the society as both symptom and
cause of the difficult situation through which Portugal is passing.
     The political, social and economic problems
facing that society are the result of the advances
of and reaction to the revolutionary process un-
leashed by the military, and specifically the Movimento das Forcas Armadas, seven years ago. Since
then, major political and social actors in Portugal have been waging a pitched battle not only over
what institutional structures should be used to encourage and channel popular participation but also
over the question of from where those structures
should draw their legitimacy.
     Many of the problems facing Portugal today
have their roots in the peculiar nature of her
transition from authoritarianism to democracy. Unlike Spain which had a controlled break with the
past, Portugal cut dramatically with the Estado
Novo, and in that rupture the military played a
dominant role. Yet, while the armed forces led the
April 1974 revolution, they, as a body, did not have
very well-defined ideas as to the direction they
wanted Portuguese society to take: this, of
course, is not what Bruneau appears to suggest when
he refers to the "complete system" toward which the

MFA (along with various other parties and groups)
wanted to move Portuguese society. As became rudely
apparent by 1975, there was not one but several
MFAs and even its most politically conscious members did not have particularly sophisticated ideas.
Indeed, one of the things about the Portuguese Communist Party (PCP) which attracted many officers
was the apparent self-confidence, the rigor and
logic of the arguments presented by that party.
Notwithstanding the case of some officers who were
clandestine members of the PCP, it is to that
phenomenon that we should look when trying to explain the remarkable influence the PCP exercised in
1974 and 1975.

The defeat of the Communist-radical MFA tandem
first in August 1975 and then decisively in November 1975 settled the question of whether some sort
of hybrid Eastern European/Third World type of
"popular democracy" would be imposed on Portuguese
society. Because the defeat was not total--there
is perhaps an ingrained aversion in the political
culture and tradition to complete and violent solu-
tions--the Communists have remained a force to be
reckoned with, particularly as they retain a clear
preponderance in the labor movement. While the
elimination of the MFA(s) as a political actor has
not meant the disappearance of a military influence
over political life, the vacuum left by that movement has been filled only with difficulty and hesitation. The parties to the right of the PCP have
not had much success in coalescing their structures
and defining their political space.

Quite rightly, Bruneau identifies the party
system in Portugal as an area which will merit
particular attention in the coming years. As Juan
Linz has noted, authoritarian regimes encourage
de-politicization and tend to coopt moderate and
liberal oppositionists. Radical elements, on the
other hand, reject the system in its entirety and
generally escape integration. These groups and
organizations tend to monopolize _real_ opposition to
the regime and emerge from its overthrow (where and
if this happens) in a strong position. This hap-
pened in Portugal where for some time after April
1974 the Communists and the military were the best
organized groups in the country. While a multipli-
city of organizations emerged in the wake of the
revolution, it would be inaccurate to describe them
as parties. Slowly, and driven by the need to compete with the PCP and MFA(s), some of them did
develop, but even the most important, the _Partido_

Socialista, struggled with only partial success against the dearth of political education and culture which was the legacy of the Estado Novo. Had the transition to democracy taken place in a less traumatic form and in a more favorable international context things might have been different, but the overthrow of the Caetano dictatorship did not coincide with or bring a period of prosperity. This and the interminable arguments taking place in Lisbon over subtle, ideological nuances during 1974-76 only served to alienate the population, encouraging a disillusion with the democratic process. The results of the survey conducted by Bruneau and his associates--particularly when so many of the respondents reflect fondly on the memories of the good old days--indicate the depth of this public apathy.

It has been the Socialist party which has been the principal victim of this drift. From early 1975 to late 1978, the PS could claim with some justice that it was the axis of democratic politics in Portugal. Today, or at least in 1979 when Bruneau conducted the survey (I believe the situation has not changed for the better since then, however), only 9 percent of those asked approved of the performance of the various governments formed under the leadership of PS Secretary General Mario Soarez. A detailed analysis of the reasons of the Socialist decline (in 1975 the party garnered 38 percent of the vote, while in 1979, it only received 27 percent) is beyond the aim of this Comment. Suffice it here to note two of the most significant elements in any such explanation. For one, the PS was unable to develop an organization which could compete effectively with the PCP. In part because it did not really exist as a party until months after April 1974; in part because of an inferiority complex many Socialist leaders and cadres carried (at least early on) with respect to the PCP; and in part because the PCP had a strong labor machine in place as the result of its penetration of the vertical corporacoes of the Estado Novo; the Socialist party absented itself from the syndical arena and never paid the sort of attention to labor issues which is so important to any serious party on the Left. The PS, moreover, showed itself unwilling during its tenure in office to address decisively the mounting economic crisis Portugal faced. This ambivalence was understandable as the party was caught in a withering crossfire between opponents to its right and left, but it was deadly.

50

Failure to implement an adequate austerity program,
to decide what sort of agrarian reform program to
support, to legislate the conditions under which
previously nationalized enterprises would be
returned to their owners thus led to the Socialist
decline.

Following a period of relative moderation
which began in the wake of the abortive November
1975 coup attempt and the miserable showing their
presidential candidate Octavio Pato made in June
1976, the Portuguese Communists have openly pursued
a strategy of polarization, aimed first at weaken-
ing and ultimately splitting the PS. Eurocommunism,
that Continental phenomenon which remains as yet
much more a wish than a reality in Italy and Spain,
has not even raised its head in the PCP which remains one of the most obdurately Stalinist and pro-
Soviet parties in Western Europe and the world.
Communist strength in Portugal today, as I have suggested earlier, comes principally from its presence
in and hegemony over the labor movement. Elector-
ally, the PCP has improved over the last few years,
consolidating its majority among the agricultural
proletariat in the Alentejo and even overtaking
the Socialist party in the Lisbon district. Nevertheless, the Communists are by no means the immediate or direct threat to democracy that they were
in 1974-1975. Then, their party rode (some would
say found itself dragged along) the crest of a revolutionary wave; today, the democratic and anti-democratic Left is by and large in retreat and the most
serious threat to the constitutional order comes
from the extreme Right.

On the Right too, there can be found a potent
anti-Socialist dimension. To be sure, not all who
support or who are active in the present ruling
coalition of three parties known as the Alianca
Democratica seek a strategy of polarization and the
decomposition of the PS. Instead, many would agree
as to the importance for the stability of the system of a strong, democratic party on the Left.
Nevertheless, some who have the ear of Premier Fran-
cisco Sa Carneiro view the PS as an ineffective
party, one destined to fail and to wither away as
democracy is consolidated. Although minoritarian
still, those views may grow in weight if the
polarization of Portuguese society proceeds apace.

In the meantime, the strategy of the Alianca
Democratica is two-pronged, aiming first for a
clear majority in the October 1980 parliamentary
contest and then for the defeat of President Ramlho

Eanes in the presidential contest scheduled shortly thereafter. The latter must come sixty days after the legislative test and thirty days before the expiration of the presidential term. Victory in the parliamentary races would enable the AD to alter the Constitution such that the national Charter, drafted, as Bruneau points out, in 1976 and with a marked socialist thrust, can be amended not by a two-thirds majority in the Parliament (as is the present requirement) but rather by referendum. It would also coincide, in the best of all worlds as far as AD is concerned, with a triumph over Eanes in the presidential contest. To that end, the coalition has supported another general rank officer, Sousa Carneiro, for the office.

The strategy designed by Sa Carneiro and his supporters aims at the consolidation of AD's still rather shaky hold on the Portuguese government and at definitively pushing the military out of politics. To succeed, Sa Carneiro needs at the very least to win a parliamentary majority. If he does not attain that objective, his fragile governmental coalition may itself fall apart. Even if the AD wins, however, the road is not clear for Sa Carneiro. Supported by the Socialists, Eanes may well win the presidential election; and given the strong, Gaullist tone of the Constitution as it pertains to the Executive, he too would be well-placed.

And here we come to the most interesting aspects of Portuguese politics today. While Eanes' power rests on the continuing important role of the military, this is not the military of 1974-1975. If not vanquished, the MFA has at least been relegated to the status of a cultural residue. The idea of democracy it brought, or at least allowed to germinate, has become part of a more general patrimony which "professional" military men like Eanes seek to defend. That role remains a relevant one. Not only despite but because of the vicissitudes of the recent past, the military will play a vitally important role in the consolidation of Portuguese democracy. Their lack of political and ideological coherence, not to say immaturity, led to many of the present difficulties, but the armed forces now have a second chance. It is to be hoped that they will prove to be up to the task this time around.

2
The Economic Consequences
of the April 25th Revolution

Paul Krugman
Jorge Braga de Macedo

"Les à - coups d'acceleration de l'histoire marquent la vie des peuples comme les sacrements celle du chrétien. Ces periodes extraordinaires sont aussi la bibliothèque où, qui en a compris la grammaire, peut lire à livre ouvert les lois du changement social profond"**Serge-Christophe Kolm, La Transition Socialiste--La Politique Economique de Gauche, Paris: Les Edition du Cerf, 1977.

"In the study of social phenomena, disorder is, it is true, the sole substitute for the controlled experiments of the natural sciences. But it sometimes happens that, in the midst of disorder, events move so rapidly that we are not able properly to observe them; disorder may be excessive even to the most detached of scientists." Frank D. Graham, Exchange, Prices, and Production in Hyper-Inflation: Germany, 1920-23, Princeton: Princeton University Press, 1930.

---

*An earlier draft of this essay was presented at the II International Meeting on Modern Portugal, University of New Hampshire, June 1979.

**The sudden accelerations of history mark the lives of peoples like the sacraments mark the life of a Christian. These extraordinary periods are also the library where those who understood the grammar can read as in an open book the laws of deep social change.

In the last few years, a unique combination of drastic internal and external shocks has turned Portugal into a testing ground for social and economic theories. But the ground is dangerous; nations are not laboratories where the effects of different factors can be studied in isolation. If there are lessons to be learned from Portugal's experience, they must be based on a theoretical framework which enables one to disentangle events in which several forces operated simultaneously.

In this paper we present an interpretation of the economic experience of Portugal since the revolution. We believe that the enduring consequence of April 25 has been the transformation of Portugal into what one might call a politicized market economy. In any market economy prices of goods and factors perform the dual role of allocating resources and determining the distribution of incomes. A politicized market economy is one in which the distributional role of prices becomes a justification for their manipulation, but in which the allocative role of prices is not replaced by a centralized allocation of quantities. Examples of the resulting dilemma are presented even in relatively non-interventionist countries: e.g. the problems of EEC agricultural prices or United States oil prices. But in Portugal the dilemma has economy-wide consequences for the crucial politicized price is the price of labor.

The real wage determines the distribution of income between capital and labor, yet it is also a price determining supply and demand. If the real wage is left to the market, it may not settle at a level which is regarded as just; if it is set politically, it will not fulfill its allocative role.

The paper is organized as follows: Section 1 gives some background on Portuguese economic development before the revolution. Section 2 develops an analytical framework based on two "strategic variables"--output and the real wage--whose evolution is analyzed in Sections 3 and 4 respectively. A brief conclusion appears in Section 5.

1. BACKGROUND: PORTUGAL BEFORE 1974

In 1973 Portugal's economy was fairly typical of the group of middle income nations sometimes referred to as newly industrializing countries or "nics."[1] These countries were able to achieve rapid

economic growth during the 1960s and early 1970s
via increased trade, exploiting their relatively
abundant supplies of semiskilled industrial
workers in textbook fashion: exporting labor-
intensive manufactured goods, and also exporting
labor directly in the form of emigrant workers.
Portugal, with its 700,000 emigrant workers, relied
more than most nics on direct export of labor, but
substantial exports of textiles, electronic components, and other labor intensive manufactures had
also emerged by the early 70s.

Table 2.1 presents some statistics on Portuguese economic growth before 1974, with related
statistics of Spain and Greece for comparison. All
three countries grew in somewhat similar fashion,
so that these "soft underbelly" countries form a
natural group. Several points stand out. First,
growth was quite rapid, with real GDP per capita
growing at rates which, if not up to South Korean
or Taiwanese standards, were still much higher than
less developed countries in general have managed.
Second, growth was pro-trade biased. In all of the
countries exports and imports rose relatively to
gross domestic product--i.e., the economies became
more "open" as they grew. In 1974-77 Portugal
diverged from the others: Spain and Greece continued to grow more open, while Portugal did not.

In saying that Portugal achieved fairly rapid
growth, we are not implying that all was for the
best. In a sense, during these years of growth,
Portugal moved into an economic relationship with
industrial Europe similar to that of Puerto Rico
with the mainland of the United States. Portugal
became a dependent economy. Such "dependence" need
not be interpreted in a Marxist way, certainly not
in a way that suggests that what was happening was
economically bad for Portugal. The problem was
(and is) simply that Portugal's economy is strongly
affected by economic policy decisions of the
industrial countries, decisions in which it has no
voice.

The other problem with Portuguese growth was
distributional. While it is probably true that
nearly all Portuguese gained from growth, the gains
were distributed unequally, both between city and
countryside, and between the population at large
and the elites which controlled economic and
political life. There is little hard evidence on
this, but by 1973 Portugal appeared to be a "dual-
istic" economy whose traditional sector had not
shared fully in growth.

56

TABLE 2.1
Growth in Southern Europe Before 1974

	Portugal	Spain	Greece
Rate of Growth of GDP			
Per Capital, 1968-73	7.4	5.8	7.5
Exports/GDP, 1968	24.2	13.0	9.6
Exports/GDP, 1973	25.8	14.3	14.2
Imports/GDP, 1968	29.2	15.6	18.2
Imports/GDP, 1973	33.2	15.6	25.2

Source: International Monetary Fund, International Financial Statistics.

Despite these problems, it is difficult not to
regard the Portuguese economy before 1974 as a
successful one.   To be sure, Portugal was still,
in 1973, a poor country; but it was steadily catching up with the industrial west.
This qualified success story came to an abrupt
end in the fall of 1973.   Despite her claim on the
abundant oil of Angola, the oil embargo had a
particularly strong effect on Portugal.   In February 1974 inflation shot up to an annual rate of
over 30 percent, supplies of some foodstuffs in
Lisbon were disrupted, some white collar trade
unions went on strike, and it was in a political
vacuum that an "Armed Forces Movement"--of ambiguous
economic ideology--took power on April 25.
Suddenly, then, the Portuguese economy was
subjected to a unique combination of shocks.   Political and social revolution at home, in addition to
its direct effects, triggered a massive return of
settlers from Africa.   At the same time the crisis
in the world economy raised the prices of imports,
depressed the demand for exports, and provoked a
return of emigrant workers as well.   But before
attempting, once again, to isolate a few crucial
aspects of these complex economic events, we must
first turn to a discussion of the theoretical
framework determining our choice of points to
emphasize.

2.   A FRAMEWORK FOR ANALYSIS

Our method in this paper will be to concentrate
on two "strategic" variables, the real wage rate
and the level of output; or more precisely, on output relative to potential and the real wage relative
to its "warranted" level, a concept which will be
explained below.   Other aspects of Portugal's
economy will be considered either as affecting
these strategic variables or as being affected by
them.   In other words, we will attempt to sort out
the tangle of events by first tracing the path of
the strategic variables; then working backward to
the major causes of changes in these variables; and
finally moving forward to the effects of the
changes.
The idea of concentrating on a few strategic
variables is probably worth justifying, although
this is not the place for an extended methodologi-
cal discussion.   Our basic suppositions are that,
while the number of variables which have been

58

subject to changes in recent years is large, the
number of variables which are of crucial policy
importance is fairly small. At the same time, we
suppose that some of these crucial variables can
be regarded as determined by the others, so that
the structure of the economy looks something like
this:

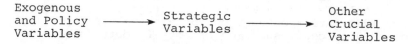

Exogenous
and Policy   ⟶   Strategic   ⟶   Other
Variables   Variables   Crucial
                                          Variables

where the strategic variables are thus both important in their own right and the intervening variables through which other important variables are
determined. Exogenous and policy variables include
oil prices, the exchange rate, government spending,
and so on; the main crucial but not strategic variables are the balance of payments, unemployment,
and the distribution of income.

The virtue of this scheme is that it allows us
to focus on a relatively limited number of channels
of cause and effect. The defect is, of course,
that it involves a simplification, and may give a
somewhat misleading transparency to events. However, when there are a few shocks as drastic as
those which Portugal has experienced, even very
simple analysis can be enlightening.

Let us begin, then, by discussing the crucial
relationships which we find in the Portuguese
economy. First, and most obvious, is the
relationship between output and unemployment.
Other things being equal, higher output will mean
higher employment, and there is some level of output which corresponds to "full employment" (including an allowance for some normal level of unemployment). Less often emphasized but also crucial is
the relationship between output and the real wage,
on the one hand, and the current account of the
balance of payments on the other. Clearly,
increasing output will swell the demand for imports
and, other things being equal, worsen the balance
of payments. Holding output constant, an increase
in the real wage will normally involve increasing
the price of domestic goods relative to foreign
goods, so that there will also be a negative effect
of the real wage on the balance of payments.

When, for simplicity, the level of output consistent with full employment is independent of the
real wage, these relationships can be illustrated
with a diagram like Figure 2.1.[2] In the diagram,

Figure 2-1
The "Zones of Economic Unhappiness"

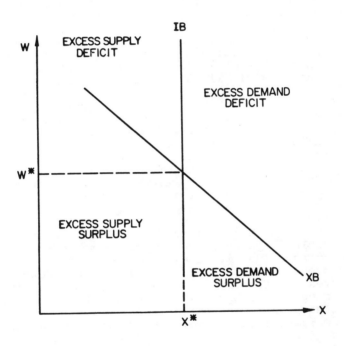

one axis measures X, the level of real output,
while the other measures the real wage rate W. The
vertical line IB indicates the level of output
consistent with full employment, while the line XB
indicates the combinations of real wage and real
output consistent with current account balance.
The diagram shows that, given full employment output X*, there is a unique level of the real wage
W*, which is consistent with external balance. We
will refer to W* and X* as the "warranted" real
wage and "potential" output respectively. They are
the only levels of W and X which are consistent
with equilibrium in both the labor and foreign
exchange markets. Departures from these levels
always involve a situation of disequilibrium--that
is, a situation of economic or social stress.

The possible kinds of disequilibrium are
illustrated by the "zones of economic unhappiness"
surrounding the equilibrium point. For each zone
the state of the labor market and of the balance
of payments are indicated. On the eve of the
revolution, Portugal was in a situation of tight
labor markets and payments surplus, i.e., it was
in the southeastern zone of the diagram. Since
late 1974 the characteristic state of the economy
has been more like that in the northwest zone--
persistent unemployment and current account
deficits.

While a diagram like Figure 2.1 is of considerable diagnostic use, it has some defects if
one tries to use it to discuss events in Portugal.
The problem is that the schedules have undoubtedly
shifted drastically. For example, by increasing
the supply of labor the arrival of the returnees
must have increased potential output and reduced
the warranted real wage. In order to trace out the
path of the economy one would not only have to keep
track of W and X but of the shifting IB and XB
schedules as well. This would destroy the simplicity of the scheme.

What we will do to avoid this problem is
replace W and X as our variable by W/W* and X/X*:
that is, by the actual values relative to their
equilibrium values. To a first approximation, one
would expect the XB and IB schedules to remain
unchanged when drawn in this space. Thus the
effect of, say, a rise in oil prices--reducing the
warranted real wage--would be to raise W/W* for a
given W, not to shift the XB curve. The variables
W/W* and X/X* become our strategic variables, and
the starting point of our analysis is a story about

their path over time which makes sense of the
observed economic developments.

This may be an appropriate place to say something about the "structural" aspect of Portugal's
economic difficulties.[3] It is often argued that
conventional macroeconomic analysis is not applicable to Portugal because the problems there are
not primarily due to increases in real wages or
domestic demand, but are instead the result of real
shocks such as the rise in oil prices and the loss
of the colonies. What this amounts to saying is
that in our Figure 2.1 the schedules have shifted;
or, equivalently, in Figure 2.2 the movement of the
economy has been due primarily to changes in W* and
X*. In fact, we would agree that such "structural"
changes have been large and important. But the
attempt to use the cause of disequilibrium to
determine the remedy is a mistake. Suppose that
external shocks--such as an oil price increase--
were to lead to a combination of balance of payments deficit and unemployment, the real wage having remained unchanged. Even though real wage
increases would not be the cause of disequilibrium,
it would still be the case that the real wage would
have to fall to achieve internal and external balance. Whatever the cause of disequilibrium, conventional macroeconomic analysis can still be used
to determine the way back to equilibrium.

Returning to the analytical framework, in
Figure 2.2 we indicate schematically the course we
believe Portugal has followed since 1973. In 1973
the Portuguese economy was in a situation of tight
labor markets, as shown by the low unemployment
rate, and was running a current account surplus;
thus our starting point, as shown in Figure 2.2, is
one of disequilibrium. There followed a series of
events which we would divide into three phases,
shown in our schematic as 1, 2, and 3.

(i) Phase 1 (1974-75): There was a rise in
real wages and a slump in output (in 1975 only).
Unemployment increased and the current account
moved into deficit. Because of the oil price
increase, the world recession, and the increase in
Portugal's labor force, the warranted real wage
dropped considerably. The last factor may also
have increased potential output. Thus we suppose
in Figure 2.2 that 1974-75 was marked by a sharp
rise in W/W*, as the numerator rose and the denominator fell, and also by a decline in X/X*.

(ii) Phase 2 (1976-77): Under pressure from
wage controls, devaluations, and the overhang of

62

Figure 2-2
Three Phases of Macroeconomic Adjustment

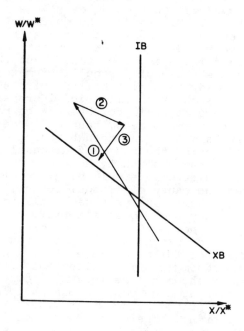

unemployed, real wages fell. But an explosion of
credit produced rapid growth in output. The effect
of output expansion was enough to worsen the
external balance in spite of the decline in real
wages.
   (iii) Phase 3 (1978-): Real wages continued
to decline; but this was now accompanied by
tightened credit, producing slower output growth.
As we show in Figure 2.2, the effect has been to
move Portugal close to external balance.

3. OUTPUT

   The evolution of output in Portugal since 1973
is summarized in Table 2.2. Until 1977 real gross
domestic product in 1975 prices grew at an average
yearly rate of 2.4 percent, much less than the
growth rates of the late 60s and early 70s but
still above the EEC figure of 1.8 percent. As is
apparent from the table, however, the variability
of Portuguese output was also higher.
   The figures for 1977 and 1978 are still first
round official estimates and some earlier figures
are included to show the precarious nature of these
estimates. First-round official estimates of 1973-
75 output available in mid-1976 were substantially
revised twice and led to underestimating the
strength of the 1976-77 recovery. Forecasts have
been even less reliable. The best 1976 forecast
for 1977 was a supposedly "optimistic" one which
assumed a 10 percent increase in investment,
regarded as extreme at the time. Yet output growth
was less than forecast.
   The plan forecast of growth for 1979 is 2.8
percent; given the rise in oil prices and the downward revisions in estimates of OECD growth, this
is probably over-optimistic.
   Chart 2.1 shows that the decline in the growth
rate in 1974 and 1975 was also accompanied by a
sharp fall in the share of output devoted to investment. This obviously tended to reduce the rate of
growth of potential output. And the investment
figure--which is in any case highly unreliable[4]--
understates the problem. A large part of capital
formation in the post 1973 period has gone to public sector projects of questionable productivity,
particularly the immense Sines project. The decline in private investment is thus far larger than
these numbers would suggest. In 1976, for instance,
public (state) investment increased by 19%, whereas

TABLE 2.2
Output Estimates (million contos)

	1973	1974	1975	1976	1977	1978	1979
1. Current prices GDP factor cost	254.2	309.0	342.1	422.6	563.8	715.4	874.8
2. GDP market prices	281.1	338.4	376.2	467.6	622.2	781.9	953.0
3. GDP in 1975 m.p. Estimated in							
3.1 1979	388.8	393.2	376.2	402.0	423.4	437.1	
3.2 1978	389.3	393.7	376.7	406.7	426.6		
Forecast in							
3.3 1976	377.8	389.0	373.5	390.3	408.0A 414.4B		
3.4 1977				383.3	397.4A 402.5B		
Growth rates % p.a.							
4. Portugal	11.9	1.1	-4.3	6.9	5.3	3.2	2.0
5. EEC average	5.9	1.6	-1.5	5.0	2.3	2.8	3.2

Sources:
1.a) 1973-76 Instituto Nacional de Estatística (except for construction in 1976, source 1.b).
 b) 1977-78 Banco de Portugal and Departamento Central de Planeamento.
 c) 1979 DCP forecast in Grandes Opções do Plano, 1979.

2.a) 1973-78 same as above.
  b) Adjusted for 1978 collected indirect taxes and 1979 budget with own estimate
     for subsidies based on same ratio to indirect taxes as 1977.

3. IFS (line 99b.p) same as 2.

3.1 1978 Banco de Portugal Report (corrected in August 1979 issue of IFS).

3.2 1977 Report.

3.3 Based on DCP numbers for 1973-75 and projection from model in A. Abel, L.M.
    Beleza, J. Frankel, R. Hill and P. Krugman, "A economia portuguesa: evolução
    recente e situação actual", in Conferencia Internacional sobre a Economia
    Portuguesa, sponsored by The German Marshall Fund of the United States and
    Fundacao Calouste Gulbenkian, Lisbon, 1977. Forecast A (pessimistic) assumes
    constant investment, B (optimistic) assumes 10% increase.

3.4 Revision 3.3 in A. Abel and L.M. Beleza, "Input-Output Pricing in a Keynesian
    Model as Applied to Portugal", Journal of Development Economics, 5, 1978.

4. From 3.1; 1979 OECD, Economic Outlook, July 1979 forecast.

5. OECD, Economic Outlook, July 1979.

66

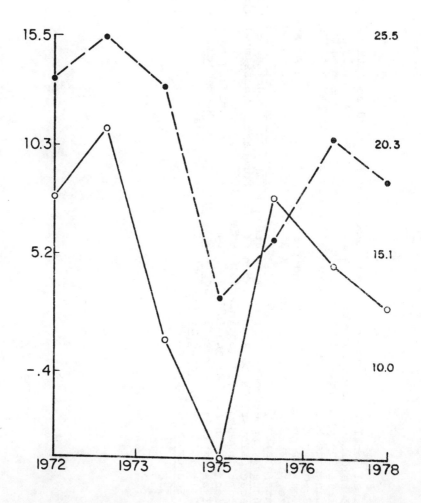

Chart 2-1

Real Growth and the Investment Share

Annual Growth Rate of Real GDP (left scale)

Real Investment Share in Real GDP (right scale)

Source: Same as Table 2.1, Line 3

housing declined by 6% and "productive" investment
(itself mainly in the nationalized firms) declined
by 6.7%, giving rise to the total decline of 3.4%.
In 1977 the 12% increase was more evenly spread
between "productive" (13.3%) and public (14.6%) but
housing continued to lag at 5.5%. Plan figures
show very little growth in investment in 1978-79.
     The effect was, apparently, a sharp reduction
in the productivity of investment. A crude but
suggestive indicator of this decline is the gross
incremental output-capital ratio, which was .41 in
1969-73 but only .13 in 1974-75. We should note,
however, that this measure of the productivity of
investment has declined worldwide. For example,
in Japan it declined from .29 in the period 1967-73
to .12 in the post 73 period. In Great Britain the
decline was from .17 to .05.
     The swings in output in Portugal were also
reflected in the crucial balance of payments.
Table 2.3 shows the changes in that balance since
1973. In 1973, as we have already mentioned, Portugal was in surplus. The deterioration in the
external environment produced an abrupt deterioration in the trade balance. Slump in 1975 temporarily reduced the demand for imports, but the boom of
1976-77 led Portugal into a severe deficit and
forced the adoption of austerity measures.
     The dramatic reversal of the external deficit
in 1978 was a definite surprise. A major part of
the improvement was a surge in emigrants' remittances, and it is possible that this was in part
dishoarding of accumulated savings held abroad as
confidence in Portugal's political stability
returned and nominal interest rates on deposits
were raised. If this is the case, remittances will
fall again, so that part of the improvement will
turn out to be only temporary. However, exports
have also surged, indicating that there has been a
fundamental improvement in competitiveness.
     The external current account is related to
national saving by the identity saving = investment + current account. It is natural, then to
consider along with the current account the public
sector deficit, which is a major source of dis-
saving as is evident from Table 2.4. In fact,
since investment has been so predominantly undertaken by the public sector, the overall deficit of
the public sector is the appropriate measure of the
gap between private savings and private investment,
where nationalized firms are included in the
private sector.

TABLE 2.3
The Balance of Payments (in millions of dollars)

	(1) Trade	(2) Current Account	(3) Non Monetary Transactions
1973	-914	351	345
1974	-2002	-829	-638
1975	-1674	-819	-1016
1976	-2115	-1246	-1179
1977	-2533	-1500	-1437
1978	-2300	-775	157
1979	-1191*	-276*	723**

Sources:
1973-1977 OECD.
    1978 Banco de Portugal,

    1979 Banco de Portugal 9/25/79 Communique and T. Cardoso, "Monetary Policy and the Balance of Payments 1976/78," paper presented at the II International Conference on the Portuguese Economy, September, 1979.

 * January-June.
** January-August.

TABLE 2·4
Public Sector Accounts (in million contos)

	(1) Current Balance	(2) Overall Balance	(3) Central Administration Budget(OGE)	(4) Balance(CGE)
1973	9.0	2.6	5.2	-2.4
1974	1.2	-7.0	8.1	-9.7
1975	-9.3	-18.5	-13.9	-25.4
1976	-13.0	-32.9	-31.8	-38.7
1977	-12.6*	-45.5*	-59.9	-49.0*
1978	-28.5*	-79.3*	-60.5	-76.6*
1979**	A-12	-62	-66.0	n.a.
	B n.a.	-113.0	-120.0	n.a.

Sources:
1973-76 Estatisticas das Finanças Publicas.
1977-78 Banco de Portugal using data from Ministerio das Finanças.
1979 A   OECD Portugal Economic Survey, July 1979,
p. 54.
     B   Revised official forecast for (3) Expresso,
10/13/79 and June ratio (2)/(3) as in A.

 * Estimates.
** Forecasts.

Chart 2.2 shows a remarkably close relationship between the external current account and the
public sector borrowing requirements, measured in
dollars. The surprising turn of the external
account in 1978 is again evident there, since the
available evidence suggests a substantial worsening
of the public sector deficit. Given the revised
budget deficit of the state, the public sector
borrowing requirement seems likely to increase
again in 1979, increasing the gap further.

In output and expenditure, then, Portugal
experienced some sizeable fluctuations. These
fluctuations were somewhat larger than those of
other European countries, and the balance of payments problem has been severe. Nonetheless, Portugal has not been too far out of line with the
experience of other semi-industrialized countries.
What makes the Portuguese experience unique are the
developments in the labor market.

Portugal in 1973 was a country with an unusually high proportion of its population working outside the country. Emigrant workers amounted to
17.5 percent of employed Portuguese in 1975. When
recession came to Europe, emigration halted and
partially reversed. At the same time, the returnees began to arrive from Africa. The result is
shown in Table 2.5: there was a huge growth in the
labor force--some 13 percent from 1973 to 1977
according to the only available estimate (source A).

Because of the growing labor force, and because
employment grew only slightly, unemployment rose to
very high levels. (We are not confident in these
figures, for reasons discussed in Section 4.) A
gap thus emerged between actual and potential output. We make an effort to measure potential output
and the output gap in Table 2.6. Several assumptions are made. First, we assume that potential
employment is 97 percent of the labor force: i.e.,
that the 3 percent unemployment of 1973 represents
"full employment". Second, we assume that the ratio
of the marginal productivity of labor to average
productivity is one-half, based on the 1973 labor
share. Thus we compute "full-employment" employment as 97 percent of total labor force, and assume
that the additional workers would have one-half of
the average product of those already employed.

The numbers produced by this rough calculation
show a large output gap, only slightly narrowed by
the 1977 boom. While the output gap is large, however, even closing it completely would still leave
the growth rate of per capita GDP since 1973 quite

Chart 2-2

Current Account and Public Sector Deficit

(million dollars)

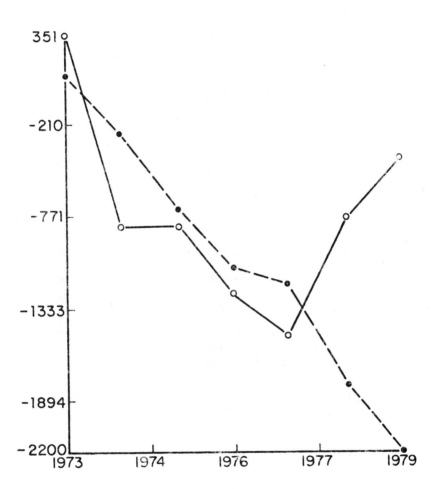

Current Account Deficit, Table 2.2, col. 2

Overall Deficit of the Public Sector, Table 2.3, col. 3

converted into dollars at average exchange rate from IFS.

TABLE 2.5
Employment and Unemployment (Thousands)

	(1) Employment			(2) Unemployment			(3) Civilian Labour Force		
	A	B	C	A	B	C	A	B	C
1973	3046	n.a.	n.a.	99	n.a.	n.a.	3145	n.a.	n.a.
1974	3061	3767	3621	180	86	47	3241	3853	3668
1975	2980	3735	3714	396	222	133	3376	3957	3847
1976	3005	3820	3759	504	276	244	3509	4096	4003
1977	3097	3781	3787	455	326	291	3552	4107	4078
1978	n.a.	3809	3736	450*	348	319	n.a.	4157	4055

Sources:
A - Gabinete de Estudos, Planeamento e Organização, Ministry of Labour as reported by Banco de Portugal.
B - INE, 1st. semester survey as reported by Banco de Portugal.
C - INE, 2nd. semester survey as reported by Banco de Portugal.

Note: (1) = (3) - (2)

* As reported in Banco Portugues do Atlântico, Conjuntura, n°12.

TABLE 2.6
Unemployment Rate and the Output Gap

	1973	1974	1975	1976	1977	1978
1. Unemployment (%)	3.1	5.6	11.7	14.4	12.8	13.0
2. Output Gap (%)	.05	1.88	4.93	6.66	5.62	5.75
3. Potential Output (million contos)	389.0	400.6	394.7	428.8	447.2	462.2

Sources:
(1) 1973-77: Table 2.5, Source A (1- (2)/(3) x 100.
     1978   : Reported in OECD (Survey, 1979) from Source A.
(2) (((1) - 3.0)/(100-(1))) x .5
(3) ((3) from Table 2.2, line 3.1) x (1 + (2)/100)

low. In other words, potential output has grown
slowly given the rise in the population. The chief
reason for this is the slow growth in productivity.
From 1973 to 1978 GDP per employee rose 10 percent,
an annual growth rate of only 1.9 percent. This
is, of course, the counterpart of the low output-
capital ratio already mentioned.[5]
     On balance, then, averaging over the fluctua-
tions, output has failed to keep up with potential,
while potential output has in turn grown disap-
pointingly slowly.

4. REAL WAGES

     The movements in the real wage in Portugal,
and the changes in the distribution of income which
accompanied these movements, are perhaps the most
striking feature of economic developments since
1973. As is shown in Table 2.7, Portuguese real
wages rose sharply in the first eighteen months
following the revolution, then began an extraordinary decline which left them, by 1978, well below
their pre-revolution level. (There are--once again
--problems with the figures, as discussed below.)
The labor share in national income paralleled this
movement, although the rise in the labor share from
1973 to 1975 was much larger in percentage terms
than the rise in real wages, so that in 1977 the
labor share was still substantially above its 1973
level.
     As we have already suggested, however, the
crucial variable from the point of view of achieving internal and external balance is not the wage
rate per se but the wage rate relative to its
"warranted" or equilibrium level. While the warranted real wage rate is not directly observable,
there can be little question that it fell sharply
in the first two years following the revolution,
for reasons discussed below. Thus, the ratio of
the actual to the warranted real wage must have
risen more steeply than the real wage itself.
Where that ratio now stands is a difficult question
which we will postpone to the end of this section.
     Let us begin by discussing the factors affect-
ing the movement of real wages since 1973. We will
then turn to a consideration of the factors which
must have affected the warranted real wage, making
an effort to put at least an order of magnitude on
the movements in this variable. Finally we will
discuss the implications of the movements in both

TABLE 2.7
Real Wages and the Terms of Trade

	1973	1974	1975	1976	1977	1978
1. Real Wage (1973 = 100)	100	106	109	101	91	89
2. Labor Share in Income (%)	51.6	57.0	68.9	66.6	60.0	56.4
3. Terms of Trade (1973 = 100)	100.0	89.9	76.8	73.2	74.9	76.0

Sources:
1973-77:   1 :   IFS.
        2,3:   Portugal: Current and Prospective Economic Trends, World Bank, November, 1978.
1978   :   1 :   INE, Boletim Mensal.
        2,3:   Banco de Portugal.

variables.

Causes of Changes in Actual Real Wages

Since 1973 wages in Portugal have been largely
a political phenomenon. The political climate
affects wage settlement directly through its impact
on bargaining and on public sector wage decisions.
At the same time, government policy plays an
important role in determining real wages through
wage and price controls, taxation, and exchange
rate policy. Market forces do have some effect,
especially in the small-business sector. But the
principal way that economic pressures affect real
wages is by inducing the government to take action
to push real wages towards a level which it regards
as appropriate.

In 1974-75 the internal situation in Portugal
naturally made for intense pressure for real wage
increases, while the "war chest" of foreign
exchange and gold left by the old regime allowed
the successive governments to ignore external
constraints for the time being. One can easily
draw up a sizable list of factors making for wage
increases. First, there were large increases in
the minimum wage. Second, wages paid by the govern-
ment--both in the traditional public sector and in
newly nationalized firms--were sharply increased.
Third, legal restrictions which were placed on
dismissals de facto forced firms to continue paying the wages of striking workers, with obvious
effects on the balance of power in wage bargaining.
Even the threat of bankruptcy was not much of a
limitation, since loss-making firms were often able
to get low-interest loans--in effect subsidies--to
cover their wage bills. Finally, the political
climate itself made for worker militancy and
employer timidity.

We should note that in addition to a redistribution of income from capital to labor there was a
redistribution within the labor force to the less
well-paid. In particular, changes in the tax
system would have made it necessary for higher-paid
workers to have received much larger percentage
wage increases to keep up with inflation than those
with lower initial wages, as shown by the figures
reproduced in Table 2.8.

The fact that nominal wage increases were in
part translated into real increases, instead of
merely being dissipated in inflation, was also
largely due to policy. For one thing, many prices

TABLE 2.8
Constant Real Take Home Pay

Equivalent Nominal Gross Wage (contos/month)		% Share in Increase	
1974	1979	Inflation	Tax
4	12.2	86.5	13.5
8	25.8	79.8	20.2
15	55.7	65.3	34.7
30	267.7	22.3	77.7

Source: BPA, Conjuntura, 12, July 1979.

Note: See also M. Cadilhe and A. Costa, "Remunerações, Inflação e Fiscalidade en Portugal: 1973 e
1977," Economia, II, 2, May 1978.

were controlled under an elaborate system insti-
tuted in 1974. This system kept cost increases
from being fully passed on in many areas,
especially in rents. Price controls were supple-
mented by subsidies used to keep down the prices
of some consumption staples. And import prices
were kept down by the Bank of Portugal's support of
the escudo.

With all of these forces working to raise real
wages, it is somewhat surprising that the real wage
index reported in Table 2.7 did not rise more. In
part this may reflect the unreliability of the
statistics,[6] but there were also some factors working to depress real wages, notably increases in
taxation and the worsening of Portugal's terms of
trade. These factors are considered below in our
discussion of movements in the warranted real wage.

From 1976 on many of the policies which had
fostered real wage increases in 1974-75 were
reversed. A catalogue of major actions would include the following: (i) ceilings were placed on
wage increases; (ii) controlled prices were raised;
(iii) the escudo was repeatedly devalued; (iv) subsidies were reduced and taxes increased; (v) labor
laws were changed so as to allow dismissals, and
(vi) the interest rates on loans to loss making
firms were increased.

In addition to these policy actions, there was
pressure on the wage rate from the overhang of
unemployed workers, swollen by returnees from
Africa and the halting of emigration to Western
Europe.

The most obvious way in which policy affected
the real wage rate is, of course, through devaluation. Devaluation--if it is effective--has the
effect of lowering the wage rate in terms of external prices. This in turn implies a fall in the
real wage in terms of imports and other tradable
goods. Chart 2.3 shows the Portuguese real wage in
terms of external prices, as measured by a weighted
average of the four principal trading partners, and
in terms of the domestic CPI. It is clear that the
large decline in the "external" real wage must have
played an important role in the decline of real
wage in terms of consumption goods.

What is surprising about the post-1976 period
is how severe the decline in real wages has been.[7]
The greater part of this decline took place under a
socialist government, in a country where trade
unions remain powerful. To make sense of such
remarkable decline, we must now consider the

Chart 2-3

Internal and External Real Wages

(1973-100)

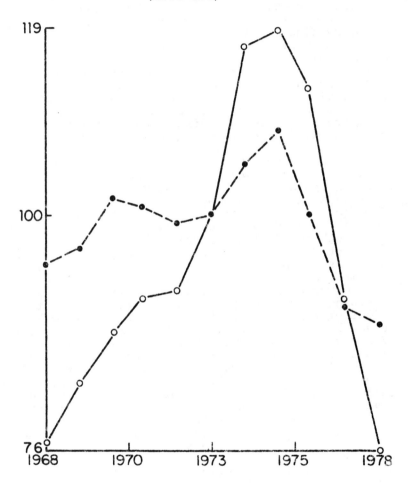

Based on the escudo CPI of four main trading partners from <u>IFS</u>; weights from Macedo (op. cit., p. 263)

Based on the Lisbon CPI including rent, Table 2.7, line 1

factors affecting the warranted real wage.

Causes of Changes in the Warranted Real Wage

Since we cannot directly observe the warranted real wage, it is necessary to attempt to infer it from indirect evidence. This evidence can be of two kinds. First, the nature of the disequilibrium a country finds itself in can be an indication of the position of the actual relative to the warranted real wage. If, for example, a country finds itself oscillating between unemployment and balance of payments deficits, this is an indication that the actual real wage exceeds the warranted. Second, one can attempt to take account of the main factors which are likely to have affected the warranted wage. We will concentrate first on this latter approach.

Factors affecting the warranted real wage may be divided into two groups. The more important of these groups is the set of "external" shocks that occurred in 1973-75 and were not under the control of policy: the rise in oil prices, the onset of economic stagnation in industrial countries, and the growth in the labor force. Probably less important but still significant were policy actions: increases in indirect taxes and in Social Security contributions.

Let us start with the external shocks. The worsening in the international environment had the effect of reducing the real income of the Portuguese nation as a whole, and therefore presumably of reducing the warranted real wage. The size of this effect was quite large: as shown in Table 2.7, Portugal's terms of trade worsened by 24 percent from 1973 to 1978, which given the 1973 import share in GDP of 33 percent implies a reduction in real national purchasing power of about 8 percent.

At the same time, returnees and returning emigrant workers from Western Europe swelled the labor force by about 13 percent. Since the capital stock was not increased accordingly--indeed, the period since the revolution has been marked by low investment--the fall in the capital-labor ratio must also have acted to depress the equilibrium real wage.

Along with these external shocks came certain government actions which acted to further lower the warranted real wage. The most easily measurable of these were the increases in indirect taxes, from 13 percent of expenditure in 1973 to 15 percent in

1978, and the increase in Social Security payments
from 11.1 to 15.1 percent of labor income. Both of
these widened the "wedge" between the price of output and the remuneration received by factors of
production.

Can we estimate the impact of these factors
on the warranted real wage? There are a number of
obstacles to any such calculation. First, there
are the measurement difficulties: not one of the
crucial numbers can be considered reliable. Second
there are technical difficulties arising from
possible changes in the equilibrium share of wages
in factor payments. If imports are a better substitute for capital than labor, the worsening in
the terms of trade would tend to raise the equilibrium labor share (and conversely); the extent to
which an increasing labor force lowers the equilibrium real wage depends on the elasticity of substitution between capital and labor.

The best we can do is to make a hypothetical
calculation which will give some indication of the
order of magnitude of the effects. Such a calculation is presented in Table 2.9. We must emphasize
that the assumptions on which the calculation is
based are extremely shaky; the true number could
easily be considerably more or less than our number. So as not to give a spurious impression of
precision, we deal only in round numbers.

The first entry is the effect of the decline
in the terms of trade. Here we assume that the
proportional reduction in the warranted real wage
is the same as the proportional reduction in real
national purchasing power as a whole. The entry
which follows is the effect of the 13 percent
increase in the labor force. Two assumptions are
made here: (i) The elasticity of substitution
between capital and labor is taken to equal one,
so that the equilibrium share of labor did not
change;[8] (ii) we use the 1973 labor share of one-
half as a measure of the elasticity of output with
respect to labor input. The result, then, is an
estimate of 6 percent for the effect on the warranted real wage. The effects of tax increases,
shown by the remaining entries, add a further 6
percent.

What is immediately apparent is that, without
any deliberate inflation of the figures, we are
able to come up with a quite large number for the
decline in the warranted real wage. In fact, if
we are concerned with the ratio of the actual to
the warranted wage, this calculation suggests that

82

TABLE 2.9
Hypothetical Calculation of Decline in Warranted
Real Wages, 1973-78

Decline in terms of trade	8 Percent
Labor force growth	6 Percent
Increase in indirect taxes	2 Percent
Increase in Social Security payments	4 Percent
Total	20 Percent
Less : Productivity increase	10 Percent
Equals: Decline in warranted real wage	10 Percent
Decline in actual real wage from Table 2.7	11 Percent

the decline in the denominator of W/W* was more important in 1973-75 than the rise in the numerator. We must repeat, however, that what we have done here is purely a suggestive calculation, not something which can be treated as a reliable estimate.

The shocks we have considered must have led to a once-for-all decline in the equilibrium real wage. Although one would generally expect this to be offset over time by the normal, secular growth in the equilibrium real wage, there are some reasons for pessimism in the case of Portugal. First, the years since 1973 have been marked by low productivity growth worldwide. Second, Portugal has had lower growth in investment since 1973 than before-- and much of the investment has, as discussed in Section 3, been devoted to public sector prospects of doubtful productivity. Finally, the institutional changes brought by the revolution have probably had at least the initial effect of hindering productivity growth. This is certainly true in agriculture, and may also be true for the nationalized firms.

We can get a rough estimate of the actual secular growth in the warranted real wage by looking at actual labor productivity. Our preferred estimate in Section 3 was that GDP per employee increased 10 percent from 1973 to 1978. But we suspect this may be too high. Official data on employment are "very heterogeneous and partially contradictory" (as generously described by the OECD). Growing employment in family enterprises, self-employment, and public administration has surely been understated.[9] Unless GDP is comparably understated (which is also possible) the productivity growth is exaggerated. In any case, even if we use the 10 percent estimate, we find that secular growth is much less than the impact decline in the warranted real wage.

The implication of this is that the warranted real wage is probably still, in 1979, below its 1973 level; 10 percent below, by our estimate. What this means for the appropriateness of the actual real wage is the next question.

The Current Situation

Data for 1978 shows a real wage in Portugal down about 20 percent from its 1975 peak. At the time, the disequilibrium state of the economy seemed to suggest that the real wage was still above its warranted level. That is, there was

still some balance of payments disequilibrium
(perhaps more than the current account indicated,
since as pointed out in Section 3 some of the
surge in emigrants' remittances may be temporary),
together with high unemployment.

As we have seen, given the size of the shocks
which have affected Portugal, it is possible that
the real wage is still too high to allow simul-
taneous balance of payments equilibrium and full
employment. It is too soon to judge, however; we
may be witnessing delayed effects of the earlier
period of high real wages.

In any case, there is no reason to believe
that the real wage is currently very far from its
warranted level. Indeed, if one compares our
estimate of the decline in the warranted real wage
with the estimated actual decline one sees that
the two are almost exactly equal. Given the
roughness of our methods, however, this seeming
exactitude is a mildly embarrassing coincidence.

5. AN ASSESSMENT

In the years since April 25th, the realistic
alternatives available to successive Portuguese
governments have all been unpleasant. For the
short run, the choice has always been between cutting real wages, increasing unemployment, and running a balance of payments deficit. As reserves
have been drawn down and foreign indebtedness has
grown, the last option has become increasingly
difficult to manage. So the last five years have
been marked by a narrowing of already binding
constraints.

The eventual direction of Portuguese policy
has thus been determined by the logic of the situation. Recent improvements in the external balance
notwithstanding, the balance of payments constraint
still precludes any sustained increase in either
real wages or employment.

Given the constraints on policy, details of
demand management are not of central importance.
The actual record on stabilization is mixed. In
1974-75, although the slump in Portugal was deeper
than in the rest of Europe, this is not surprising
given the severity of the internal and external
shocks. In fact Portugal did remarkably well; the
actions of the government, even though not con-
sciously planned, acted to support demand and limit
the initial damage.

That in 1976-77 the demand expansion, and in particular the surge in consumption and public investment, were larger than in the industrial countries--despite the overhang of the 1974-75 disturbances--was also the result in part of lack of a consistent policy but this time was clearly inappropriate. Indeed, this expansion dissipated the remnants of the "war chest" and pushed Portugal deeper into debt, eliminating whatever remained of the country's room for maneuver. More seriously, the implementation of poorly conceived investment projects in the public sector did not improve the country's prospects for long term growth.

Thus, the austerity program agreed upon with the IMF in May 1978 had to be more stringent than would have been the case, had it been implemented by the first constitutional government in the summer of 1976. Also, with rising private savings, the diversion of these savings to finance the rising deficits of the public sector and state enterprises has probably become a major cause of continuing inadequacy of private investment, an inadequacy which is an important brake on the growth of potential output and of the warranted real wage.

Real wages are at the heart of Portugal's experience in recent years. In 1974-75 a huge gap opened between the actual and the warranted real wage. Then an extraordinary decline in real wages set in, probably closing this gap. The downward flexibility of real wages in post-revolution Portugal is remarkable; the far smaller declines in the early 1970s may have been a cause of the revolution. However, the fall of the fourth constitutional government in June 1979 has been linked to the announcement of an extraordinary tax on labor income, which suggests that the downward flexibility may have a floor.

What can be learned from Portugal's experience? Perhaps the main lesson is in the "narrow limits of the possible" when one tries to redistribute income in a market economy. The allocative effects of disequilibrium real wages, manifesting themselves in a critical balance of payments problem, forced governments of pro-workers sympathies to engineer a steep decline in workers' standard of living. The dilemma of the politicized market economy could only have been eliminated by going over to a centrally planned economy. But this would have other and we believe far worse political and economic consequences.

86

NOTES

1. OECD (The Impact of the Newly Industrializing Countries on Production and Trade in Manufactures, Paris, June 1979) lists as members of the
group of newly industrializing countries the following nations: Greece, Portugal, Spain and
Yugoslavia in southern Europe; Brazil and Mexico
in Latin America; and Hong Kong, Singapore, South
Korea and Taiwan, in Asia. Note that the grouping
together of these countries is not meant to deny
the significant differences in the growth process
between, say, the "Gang of Four" in Asia and the
southern European nations.
2. This diagram draws on the well known
analysis by T. Swann, Longer-Run Problems of the
Balance of Payments, 1955, reprinted in R. Caves
and H.G. Johnson, editors, Readings in International Economics, Homewood, Ill.: Irwin, 1968,
p. 455-464 as well as the recent discussion by
F. Modigliani and T. Padoa-Schioppa, "La Politica
Economica in Una Economia con Salari Indicizzati al
100 o Piu", Moneta e Credito, 1° Trim, 1977. Allowing for a positive effect of the real wage on output would not change the analysis.
3. See Chapter 3.
4. Portuguese estimates of fixed investment
are based on sales of construction materials.
Since administrative backlogs led to lax enforce-
ment of building codes in this early post-revolution period, the composition of these sales changed,
making estimation a hit-or-miss affair. Changes in
stocks are estimated by even less reliable quess-
work.
5. Productivity calculated in this way diverges
from the estimates reported by the Banco De Portugal. In the 1977 Report, the growth of productivity
for 1976 and 1977 above was 11%. The 1976 figure,
however, was 7.1% in the 1977 Report and 3.4% in
the 1976 Report. See further estimates in J.
Macedo, Portfolio Diversification and Currency
Inconvertibility, unpublished Ph.D. dissertation,
Yale University, 1979, p. 232, note 61.
6. Thus the official figures for 1978 wage and
price inflation are based on average annual earnings in manufacturing including social security
payments and the new price index on the Continent
whereas the series used in Table 2.7 line 1 and
Chart 2.3 are the old indices of hourly wages and
the Lisbon CPI including rent reported in IFS. The
1978 increase in the latter wage and price indices

is 11% and 13% respectively, whereas the increase
in the former is 18% and 21% respectively. The use
of the Lisbon industrial wage index underestimates
return to labor because both the Oporto industrial
wage index and the agricultural index are higher,
on the other hand the use of the Lisbon CPI
including rent underestimates inflation. A
weighted average of real wages in agriculture,
men and women, Lisbon and Oporto using the respective CPI's (without rent) just about matches the
one in Table 2.7, except in 1976 and 1977 where
the values are 4 and 3 percentage points higher
respectively.

7. On the levelling-off of growth in the
internal real wage before 1974, see chapter 4,
section 6, below. The inverted J shape of the
real wage series after 1974 is used by Kolm, op.
cit., Figure 1, p. 35, to illustrate the effects
of a political victory of the right following a
political victory of the left in the cases of
Chile and Portugal. The effect of the external
shocks is however crucial: notice that the external real wage has a much more pronounced J pattern.

8. Estimates of the elasticity of substitution
between capital and labor have been made for Portugal by A. Sousa, Funções de produção com elas-
ticidade de substituição constante na industria
transformadora portuguesa, Economia, I, January 1,
1977 and M. Barbosa, Growth, Migration and the
Balance of Payments in a Small Open Economy,
unpublished Ph.D. dissertation, Yale University,
1977. Sousa's estimate was 0.6; Barbosa's 0.8.
In assuming a value of 1, we are biasing our
results toward an understatement of the decline in
the warranted real wage.

9. 1979 Survey, cit. p. 10. The three sources
indicated in Table 2.5 are not comparable with
each other. Sources B and C, which are now the
only ones used by Banco de Portugal begin in 1974
(See INE, Boletim Mensal, 1979 no. 4, supplement)
and the values of source A for 1978 are not directly available. These values are close to the ones
indicated by J. Moura, Emprego e Formação Profis-
sional Extra-Escolar no Continente, background
paper for the II International Conference on the
Portuguese Economy, September 1979, Table 4 which
include agriculture and public sector even though
the OECD Survey, p. 11 footnote 10 claims that the
Ministry of Labor poll excluded these sectors.

COMMENT

T. Sriram Aiyer

The authors present "an interpretation of the economic experience of Portugal since the revolution." The paper analyzes the two "strategic variables" output and the real wage and concludes that the real wage is at the heart of Portugal's experience in recent years. The paper also discusses the concept of the "warranted" real wage and "potential" output which are the only levels consistent with equilibrium in both the labor and foreign exchange markets. For example, the arrival of the returnees, the paper argues, should, by increasing the supply of labor, have increased potential output and reduced the warranted real wage. That this model may be a simplification is acknowledged in the paper.

The authors' model is attractive precisely because of its simplicity in the way it presents the macroeconomic variables of wages and output and the link with employment and the current account balance. While this is so, in terms of its use for economic management, it does not go far enough. For this purpose, many of the key mechanisms which remain implicit in the authors' model need to be analyzed explicitly and the bases discussed at a more micro level. Although the larger the number of explicit variables that are introduced in any model the more complex it becomes, a minimum capacity for projection into the future is essential if the model is to be useful in terms of policy. So much for general remarks.

Comments on some of the specific issues which seem to be worth examining besides real wages and output in the evolution of the Portuguese economy since 1974 are given below:

The decline in _profits_ was an important link in the succession of events leading from the increase in real wages in 1974 to their decrease in

1978-79 as well as the origin of the increased in-
debtness of many enterprises.

The disorganization of production resulted
first in a decrease in profits and then more recently in real wages. It appears that there have not
only been shifts of national income between wages
and profits, but also an overall decline in the absolute level of profits. The decrease in the
profits of enterprises placed an increased burden
on the public sector and the banking system and
resulted in almost no productive investment. For
example, the ten largest companies of the mechanical
and engineering subsector saw their rate of return
decline from 11 percent in 1973 to minus 33 percent
in 1973-76. To finance the limited amount of investment which was achieved, the enterprises of the
sector had to rely on debt. Thence the capital
structure deteriorated (from 65 percent equity in
1973 to 29 percent in 1976) and the financial
charges, guaranteed by the government, increased,
reaching 18 percent of the value of production in
1978.

Although the warranted wage rate implicitly
deals with <u>productivity</u> of labor (although perhaps
not adequately), at the micro level the productivity
of capital is also an important factor. In the
first two years immediately following the revolution
the nationalized public sector and the mixed sector
investment programs continued without account of
economic or financial criteria while those in the
private sector largely slowed down. A large part
of the capacity of the economy went unutilized
(while the employees remained in their jobs). The
productivity of capital therefore fell (see chart
2-4). However, during the past two years and
especially in 1979 the output in the economy as a
whole has risen significantly although there has
been little investment in new productive capacity
(see chart 2-5). This means that hitherto unutilized productive capacity is now being used to
increase output.

Third, <u>the role of inflation</u> in the adjustment
mechanism is not analyzed although it certainly was
a key factor in the adjustment of real wages.
Prices have increased faster since 1976 than nominal
wages and thus real wages have declined. A portion
of the inflation in Portugal can be attributed to
prices of imports, i.e., through the devaluation.
The extent to which inflation has been due to imports and that which was caused by cost push and
the increase in demand are two questions which need

91

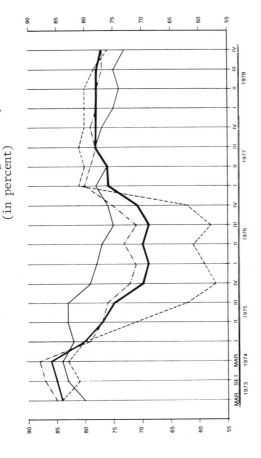

Chart 2-4: Rate of Use of the Productive Capacity
in Manufacturing Industry
(in percent)

Sources: Instituto Nacional de Estatistica,
Lisbon, and Banco de Portugal

Consumer goods -----Capital goods
-.-.- Intermediate ▬▬Total
goods

Chart 2-5: Investment in Manufacturing Industry
(deflated by GDP deflator)

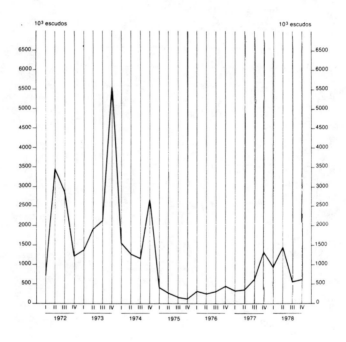

Source: Gabinete de Estudos e Planeamento do Ministerio
da Industria e Technologia; Banco de Portugal,
1979 Annual Report

to be addressed. It also seems that something could be said on the way the State managed inflation, protecting certain groups and sectors more than the others against inflation. A little more analysis is warranted on this issue.

In reality, the real wage is affected by many variables. The authors chose to select a few of them, thereby bringing out a simple and attractive model; however, the value of their analysis is limited for policy because they do not deal adequately in their analysis with such important variables as productivity and inflation. Their framework is static while the adjustment of the Portuguese economy to the revolution of 1974 is a dynamic process.

Even as a static framework the authors' presentation has technical weaknesses: the IB and XB curves are not really independent. If for example there were an increase in productivity, according to the authors this should shift the IB curve to the right. In reality it will also modify the XB curve in a way which is not predictable. Due to an increase of productivity the exports are likely to increase but due to the high import content of exports, the latter would also rise. We cannot tell whether this change will, in fact, result in a new equilibrium of the balance of payments since not only could the XB curve shift but its slope might also change. As a result the core of their argument--the existence of a unique warranted wage rate compatible with full employment and a current account balance-- cannot be clearly demonstrated. Nor does the model convincingly show that the long-run survival of Portugal's economy can be assured if real wages were used as the principal adjustable instrument. A priori, there is no reason to believe that this level exists and, if it did, to believe that it is stable. Besides the loss of the colonies, the influx of returnees, the reduction of the employment possibilities in Western Europe for Portuguese workers, and the new orientation towards export promotion, all added to the political constraint on labor management, have deeply transformed the Portuguese labor market. In other words the disequilibrium in the labor market seems to be partly structural. Even if there is downward flexibility in real wages, there could be a point at which unemployment persists even if the current account balance is positive. To analyze this problem in its full complexity, one needs a model which systematically and explicitly deals with more elements.

If, as the authors do, one thinks in terms of
partial equilibrium, the choice of the "strategic"
variables is crucial and the conclusions one
reaches depend on, and are limited by, this
choice.

It would seem that over the long run, given
the small size of Portugal's population, to enable an increase in national income and private
consumption, Portugal will have to follow a
strategy aimed at export-led growth with industry
as the leading sector.[1] For this to succeed Portuguese wages will have to be kept from rising out of
proportion with changes in labor productivity. However, the efficient use of labor, while necessary,
is not in itself sufficient; capital also must be
employed efficiently, i.e., it must be used not
only in financially profitable investments but also
those which are economically efficient, in order to
maintain and increase the competitive position of
Portuguese products in world markets. In saying
this one cannot lose sight of Portugal's forthcoming entry into the European Economic Community in
preparation for which the country should also
develop a modern industrial base where possibly
based on exploitation of local resources and market-
able products, to minimize shocks from competition
from other richer and more industrialized EEC countries to its north. As these industries entail
capital-intensive investments, the criteria for
selection should again be the efficient use of
capital using international prices. Since the
authors dwell in part on the external account, it
is worth mentioning that an increase in investment,
productivity and hence output in the agriculture
sector is something Portuguese planners cannot
ignore however difficult these may appear at first
sight.

NOTES

1. "Portugal and the EEC; Employment and Implications" by Sriram Aiyer and Shahid A. Chaudhry,
Instituto de Estudos para Desenvolvimento, December
1979, Lisbon.

COMMENT

Luis Miguel Beleza

1. The Krugman-Macedo paper is a very interesting interpretation of some economic consequences
of the Portuguese revolution. The authors delib-
erately choose to focus on a (very) small set of
crucial variables and relationships and suceed in
presenting a paper which is clear and (perhaps)
simple but not simplistic. Their attempt to quantify a few of their most important concepts is
valuable, even though--or perhaps because--their
statistical basis is at best very shaky. They quite
clearly point out some of the bitter trade-offs
faced by the successive economic authorities, namely
between unemployment, falling real wages and balance
of payments deficits. Their paper is real, in the
sense that they pay little more than lip service to
any monetary developments or inflation, and short
run in the sense that they leave growth considerations out of the picture.
2. Several criticisms could be raised as far
as the general approach of the paper is concerned.
When attention is focused on a very small number of
concepts and/or relationships there is an obvious
gain in clarity of exposition. The essential
aspects of the diagnostic and eventual (implicit?)
policy alternatives stand out much better. Yet,
such an approach "involves a simplification, and
may give a somewhat misleading transparency to
events," as the authors themselves recognize.
Others might have chosen to focus on different
variables and/or relationships, or perhaps some
new ones. For example, more could (and has been)
made out of the international recession of 1974-75
to explain Portugal's difficulties.
Working with poor data is a predicament of
any student of the Portuguese economy. Some of the
figures used in this essay are extremely unreliable.

In particular, the data of wages is quite poor indeed. Because it is so poor, perhaps too much is
drawn out of the fall in real wages after 1975.
Indeed, it is difficult to believe that real wages
have actually fallen as much as it is stated in
this paper[1]. And care has to be taken when using
the different consumer price indices to deflate
the nominal wage figures. Because rents are frozen
in all but new contracts a substantial share of
consumer spending (12.3% according to Instituto
Nacional de Estatistica consumer price index
weights) is practically frozen. This means that
real wages as defined by the nominal wage over the
consumer price index probably overstate the real
decline in living standards of wage earners[2]. In
any case it is undeniable that real wages have
been falling significantly from 1976 on[3]. And it
is certainly better to work with poor data than
with no data at all. This means that while Krugman and Macedo are right in using the wage figures
they were able to get, they could have taken these
figures less seriously then they seem to have.
There are several other figures (estimates) which
are little more than educated guesses (i.e.,
figures on the "warranted wage"). However, in
general, the authors do not make more of them than
they should. All in all their efforts to quantify
the most important concepts seem quite successful.
The implications of their figures is clear and
probably correct, in spite of the fact that some
of their quantitative findings are questionable.
        Accelerating inflation has been a charac-
teristic of the Portuguese economy from 1974 on,
and deserved more attention than it receives here,
if for no other reason than its political impact[4].
Finally, because Portugal is at best an industrializing country, we would have liked to have seen
some analysis, however brief, of the growth prospects as they were affected by the Revolution.
        3. The basic hypothesis of this essay is
questionable: An increase in the real wage does
not have to lead to a deterioration of the external
current account. Indeed, in another paper[5] Macedo
has explained why this may not be so with the help
of some econometrics evidence that casts doubt on
the hypothesis presented here. Pentti Kouri
shows that a devaluation and a consequent fall in
the real wage may lead to a deterioration of the
current account if the (negative) effect of the
income and saving expansion it leads to outweighs
the (positive) effect on the increased supply of

traded goods.[6] James Tobin (together with Macedo)
and Macedo again show that the problem should be
analysed in the context of a more general portfolio
allocation model, where agents' preferences for
domestic and foreign assets are taken into account.[7]
In summary, the negative relationship between the
real wage and the balance of payments is not a
logical necessity of "sound" economics but at most
a working hypothesis.

We believe that such an hypothesis should
indeed be accepted for post-revolutionary Portugal.
It is quite difficult to test the hypothesis
econometrically due to the small sample size. But
the available data[8] does indicate that the fall in
the real wage--or its counterpart, the increase in
the (relative) price of traded goods--came together
with a clear increase in the relative output of
traded goods after 1977. The implied lag-real wages
in manufacturing began to fall after 1976[9]--is not
implausibly large. This increase in the output of
traded goods in 1978 and, it seems, even more
strongly in 1979, accompanied a spectacular improvement in the current account ($-1.5 billion in
1977, -.8 in 1978 and about +.1 in 1979). However,
in 1978 a series of strict expenditure reducing
measures and several measures to make domestic
financial assets more attractive were implemented[10]
--which makes it difficult to identify the effect
of the fall in real wages. In sum, while neither
economic theory nor the figures available in the
specific case of Portugal lead to the definitive
conclusion that falling real wages are associated
with improving current account, argument presented
here seems nonetheless plausible enough to be
accepted.

4. The trade-off between real wages and the
balance of payments, or employment and the balance
of payments, may be clarified if we distinguish
explicitly the traded and non-traded sectors of
the economy. This is done in Figure 2-3. It is
assumed that (domestic) aggregate demand (and
demand for labor in the non-traded goods sector)
is determined by the economic policy authority. In
the north-east quadrant we represent the combination
of the real wage (W) and an index of the level of
economic policy (D) that lead to a given value of
the external current account (B). It is negatively
sloped: a higher level of D (i.e., more expansionary monetary policy) leads to an increase in
demand, therefore to a worsening of the current
account. A lower real wage is needed to increase

Figure 2-3

Real Wages and the Balance of Payments

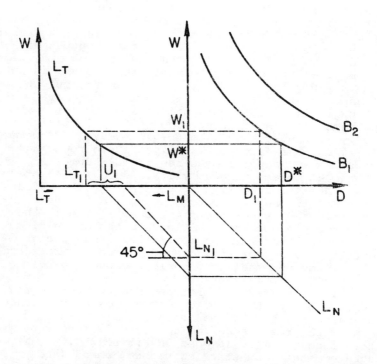

the supply of traded goods. A lower real wage also
means a higher relative price and thus lower demand
for traded goods--restore the previous value of B.
In the south east quadrant we represent the demand
for labor in the non-traded goods sector (L_N). It
is positively sloped: a higher D means a higher
level of activity, therefore higher demand for
labor in the non-traded sector. In the southwest
quadrant we simply move the value of L_N to the
horizontal axis of the north-west quadrant. The
length of the horizontal axis of the north-west
quadrant measures the domestic labor force. Demand
for labor in the traded goods sector (L_T) is
measured from left to right; from right to left
we measure L_N. On the vertical axis we have the
real wage, W. Demand for L_T is negatively sloped:
with (international) prices given, a higher real
wage means lower L_T.
            The figure works as follows. Assume that
the economic policy authority chooses a level of
B, say B_1 (Note that $B_2 > B_1$ in the figure). It
then may choose one combination of W, D that lead
to B_1. However if it is too high relative to the
"warranted wage", then the implied D leads to a
level of L_N which is too low to ensure full employment. In the picture, if $W=W_1$, D equals D_1, which
leads to L_{N1}. In the north-west quadrant we can
read unemployment, U_1. If, on the other hand,
$W=W^*$ (the warranted wage) then with $D=D^*$ we have
current account equilibrium (i.e., $B=B_1$) and full
employment. Several developments that followed
the Portuguese revolution can be read directly from
the figure. For example, the worsening of the
terms of trade and the increased supply of labor,
which move the B curves down and to the left and
increase the length of the horizontal axis of the
north-west quadrant can be seen to lower the
warranted wage.

NOTES

    1. Different, more reliable wage indices are
now available from Banco de Portugal.
    2. This is true regardless of using the old
Lisbon CPI that includes rent or the new nationwide
index which, as yet, does not.
    3. For manufacturing the New Banco de Portugal
figures show stagnant real wages in 1976 as compared to 1975, and a decline thereafter.
    4. Like in the latest (December 2, 1979)

election?

5. See Jorge de Macedo "Portugal and Europe: Crawl or Float?", presented to a Conference on "Portugal and the Enlargement of the European Community", Lisbon, January 29, 1980.

6. See P. Kouri "Profitability and Growth in a Small-Open Economy", in A. Lindbeck (ed) - <u>Inflation and Unemployment in Small Open Economies</u>, Amsterdam, North Holland Co., 1979. This is quoted in Macedo, "Portugal and Europe . . .", op. cit.

7. See J. Tobin and J. Macedo, "The Short Run Macroeconomics of Flexible Exchange Rates: An Exposition". Cowles Foundation. Discussion Paper no. 522, Yale University, April 1979, and J. Macedo "Portugal and Europe: . . .", op. cit.

8. See M. Barbosa and L. Beleza "External Disequilibrium in Portugal, 1975-78", in II Conferencia Internacional sobre a Economia Portuguesa, Lisboa, 1979.

9. According to the new series already mentioned.

10. Like tight credit controls and steep interest rate increases.

3
Portugal and the IMF: The Political Economy of Stabilization

Barbara Stallings

In 1975, it looked like Portugal might become the first socialist state in Western Europe. In 1980, the country has a right-wing free-enterprise government. This drastic change was closely connected to the economic disequilibria (balance of payments deficits and inflation) resulting from the way in which the revolutionary regime attempted to redistribute income and power. The social democrats who were elected in 1976, and their independent technocratic successors in 1978-79, took advantage of the subsequent economic chaos to justify dismantling their predecessors' structural reforms and to have the workers bear the principal burden of stabilization.

Controlling disequilibria can be important in both economic and political terms. Not only do uncontrolled disequilibria tend to undermine a government's economic policies, they may also provide fertile ground for political opposition as well. Neither a capitalist nor a socialist government can operate under conditions of rampant disequilibrium--although the idea that these can be totally eliminated is no less unrealistic since a developing economy always tends to be in disequilibrium. Thus, the question becomes one of method. How is stabilization to be achieved? Is stabilization a goal in itself, or is it part of a long-term growth strategy? Who pays the costs of stabilization? In the Portuguese case, decisions regarding such questions were influenced by, and legitimated by, the International Monetary Fund (IMF) which was an active participant in economic policy making from 1976 through 1979.

This paper will attempt to analyze the role of the IMF in the political-economic changes in Portugal over the last few years. After a few

introductory comments on the Fund itself, this
analysis will proceed on the basis of several distinct historical stages: (1) the pre-revolutionary
period; (2) the move toward socialism; and (3) the
return toward capitalism, subdivided according to
the three rounds of negotiations with the IMF
(1976-77, 1977-78, and 1978-79). Finally, the
concluding sections will discuss alternative
methods of stabilization, especially the role of
stabilization in long-term development strategies.
In this context, the British/Italian debate on deflation, devaluation, and import controls will be
introduced and related to the Portuguese case.

1.   THE ROLE OF THE IMF

The main goal of the International Monetary
Fund, as outlined in the 1945 Articles of Agreement,
was to promote an open international economy. Restrictions on free trade and restrictions on the
movement of capital were to be firmly opposed.
Subsidiary goals--necessary for the functioning of
the open economy--were promotion of monetary cooperation, a multilateral payments system, exchange
stability, and smooth adjustments of balance of
payments equilibrium.[1] It was only a few years
later that some economists realized that inflation
could interfere with the achievement of these
original goals. The 1948 Annual Report dealt specifically with this issue, and measures to control
inflation began to be incorporated into the programs set out by the Fund.[2]
In historical terms, it is clear that governments go to the Fund for one main reason--balance
of payments crises. The IMF itself has small
amounts of money to lend out, but much more important has been its role of lynchpin for the international lending system. That is, the IMF "seal of
approval" has been required by other lenders before they will provide a government with credit.
In the 1950s and 1960s, such loans came mainly from
public sources--the World Bank and bilateral agencies, especially the United States Agency for International Development and its predecessors. In the
1970s, the most important source of loans became
the private banks which, following an initial
attempt to monitor economies themselves, also came
to link their loans to IMF programs.[3]
How does a country obtain the IMF seal of approval? The process is quite standard. Top

economic officials of the country in question negotiate a stabilization program with Fund representatives, and this program is then embodied in a
"letter of intent" addressed to the IMF managing
director and signed by the country's finance
minister. The elements of a stabilization program
generally include devaluation, cuts in the budget
deficit (usually by cutting spending but sometimes
by raising taxes), cuts in credit expansion and
higher interest rates, elimination or lowering of
price controls, and the imposition of wage ceilings. The goals mentioned, however, are not all of
equal importance. Some represent the country's own
intentions over the period. Others are official
"performance criteria," meaning that if they are
not met, the loan which accompanies the stabilization program will be cut off. The targets selected
as performance criteria are those that the IMF
thinks the finance and central bank officials can
actually control. Thus, the targets normally deal
with (1) domestic credit expansion, (2) the fiscal
budget deficit, and (3) the current account of the
balance of payments. Contrary to popular opinion,
wages, either real or nominal, have never been
targeted as a performance criterion, and a specific
inflation target has been used only once (the inflation index connected to increases in the scala
mobile in the Italian negotiations of 1976-77).
Items such as increases in interest rates and devaluations tend to be prerequisites before serious
negotiations will be carried out.[4]
     The Fund refuses to publish, and in some cases
even to admit the existence of, an economic model
behind its programs. Various attempts have been
made, however, to reconstruct this model, including
one for the Portuguese case.[5] The result is an
interesting mixture of monetarist and Keynesian
relationships which is probably an accurate reflection of the theoretical eclecticism that seems to
exist in the area departments of the Fund, that is
to say those departments actually in charge of
negotiating with member governments.[6] The model is
important because it reveals certain implicit targets in the programs as well as the explicit ones.
First, there is an implicit real growth (and therefore unemployment) target. Nominal growth will be
determined by demand management (especially credit
and fiscal policy), but real growth will be determined by inflation. According to the model, inflation is a function of two variables--nominal wage
increases and import price increases. The latter,

in turn, is a function of international price movements and the exchange rate. Second, real wages
also emerge as an implicit target. The government
is allowed to name (almost) any figure it thinks
politically expedient for nominal wage increases;
real wages will then be controlled by the exchange
rate. Thus, devaluation serves multiple functions;
while it may have some effect on improving the
balance of trade, its more important role is to
regulate real growth rates and real wages.[7]

In theory, there are three ways of resolving
a balance of payments crisis: deflation, devaluation, and controls. The charter and the ideology
of the Fund, however, are firmly opposed to the
third option. Thus the possibilities offered to a
government are deflation and devaluation; the
choice is supposedly made according to which negative effects the government feels most able to deal
with--falling wages or unemployment.[8] The deflation
option works through cutting demand (credit and
government spending) which leads to lower growth
and therefore unemployment. Wages for those still
working could be unaffected. Imports fall because
of lack of purchasing power due to unemployment and
bankruptcies. Devaluation, on the other hand,
operates through changing relative prices in favor
of domestic goods. Imports fall because their
prices are higher, but domestic production may
actually increase. Inflation will also increase,
thus leading to lower real wages. In this case,
employment could be unaffected or even increase.

The third option, which the IMF tries to play
down but which governments tend to favor, is controls (on imports, prices, and/or foreign exchange
movements). Import controls operate in a way
similar to devaluation. Domestic production is
stimulated because imports are restricted, but in
this case it is by plan not market factors. The
difference is that real wages need not be cut because there is no devaluation to produce an increase
in inflation. IMF and other free trade economists
will argue that inflation is only being temporarily
suppressed, and at the cost of introducing distortions in the allocation of resources, but all of
these issues are currently being debated.[9] Bowing
to reality, an IMF-approved stabilization program
will usually have elements of all three options,
with promises for the third to be phased out.

In addition to economic policy measures, IMF
programs have structural components as well. As
with policy measures, these may be explicit or

implicit, but the content tends to be the same. That is, the Fund pushes toward less government intervention in the economy and greater reliance on market mechanisms. This, of course, is the domestic equivalent of the open economic stance they advocate at the international level. Furthermore, in addition to emphasizing private capital in general, there is also a stress on the need for foreign capital in particular. The policy measures only make sense in terms of development if they are seen as a way of attracting foreign investment. If one questions whether foreign investment can ever produce development, the IMF's programs are then left as account balancing for its own sake (at best) or a straight hindrance to development (at worst).

Stabilization programs vary in severity, depending in part on how large a loan the country is requesting in relation to its drawing rights in the Fund. (Other reasons will be discussed below.) That is, each country has a quota representing the amount it has paid in and therefore can borrow. The first 25 percent--the so-called gold tranche-- can be drawn at will. The second 25 percent--the first credit tranche--can only be drawn after a Fund mission has examined a country's economy and approved the general policy lines being followed. Further drawings carry much stricter requirements, including precise performance criteria to be met.

Four types of effects typically result from a stabilization program. First is a recession as demand falls because of lower wages, lower government spending, and lower credit. Second is the temporary easing of the balance of payments crisis because of a drop in imports due to recessionary conditions and possibly an increase in exports. Third, inflation often increases in spite of the avowed intention to slow it down. Fourth is a shift in income from wage earners toward capital because of wage ceilings and the lifting of price controls.

This is not to say that some capitalists-- mainly small ones--will not be hurt as well through falling demand, higher interest rates, and limits on credit. But chief beneficiaries tend to be foreign capitalists as restrictions on their activities are lifted, and some of their competition is driven out of business. Because of the international scale of their operations, they can get credit in other markets and sell elsewhere as well until better times return. Domestic firms do not have this alternative.

It would be a mistake, however to see this process as one where the IMF is simply trying to help the rich and hurt the poor. Rather the proper context sees the Fund as an organization that believes the capitalist system offers the greatest advantages for all. The aim is therefore to make the economy "healthy" again so that private capitalists will invest. The only way to do this is to insure that high profits will be earned, and thus it is workers who must be squeezed in order to eliminate exchange crises and inflation.

It would also be a mistake to see the IMF as unilaterally imposing stabilization programs on governments that are totally opposed to such policies. Fund officials realize that a program imposed from the outside is extremely difficult to enforce and is not likely to succeed. Rather what happens is usually a coalition between the IMF team and certain factions of the government and the bourgeoisie of the country concerned. Under such circumstances, the IMF plays several roles. It can bolster the forces of domestic groups desiring stabilization-type policies. It can also be used as a type of "scapegoat" for the negative effects such policies will produce. And the Fund can provide access to money that can then be used to partially offset these negative effects in the short run, by spreading them over a longer period of time. Let us now examine how these characteristics of the IMF manifested themselves in the Portuguese context.

2. THE PRE-REVOLUTIONARY PERIOD

The Portuguese economy under the Salazar/ Caetano dictatorship appeared to be a success-- growth rates were high, unemployment was low, inflation rates were low, and the balance of payments was in surplus. Thus, Portugal had no reason to approach the IMF. A glance beneath the surface, however, reveals the superficial nature of the "success".

In spite of its rapid growth since World War II, Portugal remained the most backward country in Western Europe. Per capita income during the last year of the dictatorship (1973) amounted to $1,350, compared to $4,500 for the OECD as a whole.[10] Sixty percent of non-agricultural workers had monthly incomes of less than $160.[11] Infant mortality rates were highest and educational levels lowest in

Europe. In structural terms, Portugal's underdevelopment could be seen in the fact that 28 percent of the workforce was still in agriculture.[12]

National income was also distributed in a
highly uneven manner in geographical, sectoral, and
class terms. Although most agricultural land in
the north was held in fairly small units, the south
was characterized by very large estates and land-
less workers. Productivity and income also varied
across sectors, with agriculture far behind industry and even services.[13] Most conspicuous was the
domination of the entire economy by a small number
of conglomerates, most of them associated with
important banking houses. These groups dominated
such varying sectors of the economy as banking,
insurance, steel, petrochemicals, paper, auto-
mobiles, electronics, and shipping. Under the
dictatorship, these groups were very closely af-
filiated with the state, and enjoyed protection and
privileges of various kinds.[14]

Another aspect of inequality concerned unemployment. On the surface Portugal had no unemployment problem, but in reality the country was unable
to provide work for its own people. There were
700,000 emigrant workers out of a labor force of
three million; if families were included, 1.5 million of Portugal's nine million people were abroad.
This does not include the tens of thousands who
were fighting the colonial wars in Africa. Clearly
unemployment would have been rampant if Europe and
Africa had not provided outlets. In addition, a
large percentage of the work force was underem-
ployed. Over one-quarter was employed in agriculture and other primary sector activities, but only
16 percent of GNP originated there.[15]

These trends were also relevant to the balance
of payments. Emigrants' remittances had been a key
factor in maintaining a positive balance in the
current account in spite of chronic deficits in
the trade balance. Thus, in effect, a major Portuguese export was people. The colonial war was
also, on balance, positive for the current account.
The captive markets and cheap raw materials more
than offset military and administrative expenses
in maintaining the empire.[16] In addition to a
positive current account, the capital account was
also in surplus as foreign capital flowed in to
take advantage of cheap Portuguese labor. (As
might be expected, there were close connections
between foreign capital and the domestic conglomerates.) Thus the old regime piled up reserves,

especially gold.[17]

By 1973-74, however, problems had begun, i.e.,
before the revolution of April 1974. The oil
price rises were a serious jolt to Portugal which
imported most of its oil. Food imports were also
reaching significant levels, as a legacy of the
neglect of agriculture over the years. In 1970,
Portugal became a net food importer for the first
time; the tendency increased through 1973.[18] Inflation began to rise during the 1970s and especially in 1973 and the first quarter of 1974, with food
up by 30 percent during the twelve months ending in
March 1974.[19] Unemployment was also picking up as
some of the emigrant workers were turned out of
Europe. In general, the worldwide economic problems were just entering Portugal as the revolution
took place.

3. THE APRIL REVOLUTION AND THE MOVE TOWARD
    SOCIALISM

The Armed Forces Movement (MFA) which overthrew the Caetano regime in April 1974 was basically a political movement. The MFA was primarily
interested in ending the dictatorship, moving toward
democracy, and--above all--ending the colonial war
in Africa. In economic terms, there were vague
goals of greater development and equality, but no
exact strategy was worked out. In fact, a precise
strategy would have been difficult to work out because of the disparate elements making up the MFA,
ranging from committed socialists to equally committed capitalists. The situation was made somewhat clearer after General António de Spínola, first
head of the revolutionary government, was thrown
out in September 1974 and the Communist Party (PCP)
began to take a more active role in the process.
It was then that the so-called "flower revolution"
became firmly linked with the goal of establishing
socialism in Portugal.[20]

The economic steps that were taken had both
short-term policy aspects and longer-run structural
components. The most important actions of the
former type were an increase in wages and public
expenditure. Nominal wages increased dramatically
in comparison with previous years; an average of
approximately 35 percent in 1974; and about 25 percent in 1975 (the previous five years had averaged
about 10 percent). Inflation also increased, of
course, but as Table 3.1 shows, real wages nevertheless rose significantly during both years. This

TABLE 3.1
Changes in Wages and Prices, 1973-78

	1973	1974	1975	1976	1977	1978
Nominal wages						
Ind. & transport						
Lisbon	13.9%	32.3%	18.7%	11.9%	12.0%	11.0%
Oporto	9.8	38.5	27.9	11.4	12.2	9.4
Agriculture						
Men	12.8	32.9	24.3	14.5	14.7	17.5
Women	15.8	40.5	34.7	13.5	19.0	12.8
Real wages						
Ind. & transport						
Lisbon	0.9	5.8	2.9	-7.6	-9.6	-9.5
Oporto	-1.1	9.2	8.6	-5.7	-11.3	-10.7
Agriculture						
Men	0.1	5.5	6.8	-4.7	-7.9	-4.1
Women	2.8	11.5	15.7	-5.6	-4.4	-8.1
Consumer prices*	11.5	29.2	20.4	19.2	27.2	22.6

Source: Banco de Portugal, Indicadores Económicos, 1973-77, p. 3; OECD, Economic
Surveys: Portugal, July 1977, pp. 14, 60-61.

* Lisbon through 1976, new national index from 1977.

was achieved through price controls, a pegged
exchange rate, and subsidies. There were also
attempts to improve the equality of the wage
structure by introducing a minimum wage in both
industry and agriculture and by freezing wages at
higher levels.

The rise in public expenditure was also important. In nominal terms, current increases were
40 percent in 1974 and 34 percent in 1975, compared
with an average of 12 percent over the previous
five years; in real terms, this meant a 28 percent
increase in 1974-75. Revenues also increased but
not nearly as fast, so that the current account was
barely positive in 1974 and heavily into the red in
1975. Adding in capital expenditures, there was a
deficit of escudos 6 billion ($240 million) in 1974
and escudos 20 billion ($740 million) in 1975 as
can be seen in Table 3.2. These deficits were almost completely covered by domestic borrowing.

The rise in demand from wage and public expenditure increases (and credit as well) meant that
output fared well in comparison to other OECD countries. There was a 2 percent increase in GDP in
1974 and a 4 percent drop in 1975. Industrial
growth increased by 25 percent in 1974 and fell by
only 5 percent in 1975. All figures are better than
those for the major industrial countries.[21] Even
if Portugal did well in relative terms, however, the
growth rates were certainly inadequate to meet the
sudden increase in the labor force. This increase
occurred for three reasons. First, the soldiers
who had been fighting in Africa came home. Second,
many of the Portuguese citizens who had been living
in Africa also returned, amounting to an estimated
400,000 people. Third, as recession hit the European countries, the doors closed to emigration. By
1975, unemployment was estimated at over 11 percent
of the workforce.[22]

The economic trend that is most relevant for
the analysis of the IMF role in Portugal was the
appearance of a balance of payments deficit. This
can be seen in Table 3.3. The deficit was partly
a result of running the economy at a higher growth
rate than other countries, but many other factors
were at work as well. Oil price increases and the
end of the empire both wracked havoc on the trade
balance. A slowdown in tourism and emigrant remittances did the same with the service and transfer
balance. Thus, for the first time in many years,
the current account went into deficit. Capital
flight exacerbated the problem as did a decline in

TABLE 3.2
General Government Expenditure and Revenue, 1973-78 (esc. bil.)

	1973	1974	1975	1976	1977	1978
Total revenue	67.6	82.3	98.2	133.8	178.9	214.0
Current revenue	63.8	77.8	93.2	131.4	173.6	211.0
Capital revenue	3.8	4.5	5.0	2.4	5.3	3.0
Total expenditures	63.7	88.1	117.1	165.0	221.9	282.0
Current expenditures	54.8	76.5	102.5	144.5	182.1	239.0
Capital expenditures	8.9	11.6	15.2	20.5	39.8	43.0
Surplus (+)/deficit (−)	3.9	−5.8	−19.5	−31.2	−43.0	−68.0

Source: Banco de Portugal, Indicadores Económicos, 1973-77, p. 5; OECD, Economic
Surveys: Portugal, July 1979, p. 32.

TABLE 3.3
Balance of Payments, 1973-78 ($ millions)

	1973	1974	1975	1976	1977	1978
Current account	$ 354	-$ 806	-$ 817	-$1244	-$1495	-$ 776
Trade balance	-920	-1948	-1671	-2109	-2531	-2315
Service balance	155	54	-183	-107	-100	-96
Transfers*	1119	1088	1037	972	1136	1635
Capital account	-144	267	-108	12	57	758
Long term private	-38	347	-21	28	28	249
Long term public	-106	-80	-87	-16	29	509
Basic balance	210	-539	-925	-1232	-1438	-18
Short term, errors/omm.	137	-91	-89	54	-57	175
Balance	347	-620	-1014	-1178	-1495	157

Source: Banco de Portugal, Indicadores Economicos, 1973-77, p. 9; OECD, Economic
Surveys: Portugal, July 1979, p. 18.

* Almost completely composed of emigrants' remittances.

long-term capital flows which actually became negative in 1975. During these first two years, the
deficit could be covered by reserves, but it was
clear that a serious problem was building up.[23]
     The structural components of the government's
economic activity were designed to move the country toward a socialist mode of production. In the
short run, however, they added to the economic
dislocations. A large-scale agrarian reform
brought some decline in output, although not nearly
as much as might have been expected based on other
countries' experiences with agrarian reform. Nevertheless, lack of experience on the part of some new
farmers, plus sabotage by those being expropriated,
drove up the food import bill. (There was also
greater consumption because of rising incomes of
the poorest groups.) Nationalization of banking
and some industrial sectors were two other key aspects of the government's strategy. This brought
on an investment boycott by the private sector and
drove up government expenditures at the same time.
The government role in the economy, in terms of
percentage of GNP accounted for by government
expenditure and government percentage of investment, both rose dramatically.[24] All of these
changes increased the government's potential control over the economy, but it was clear that actual
control, via socialist planning, was still far in
the future.

4.   THE SOCIALIST PARTY AND THE RETURN TOWARD
     CAPITALISM

The IMF Round I: 1976-77

     The year 1976 was the benchmark in the Portu-
guese Revolution. The April election for the Assembly of the Republic, and the Presidential election in June, set the stage for the retreat from
the socialist goals and pro-labor policies of the
previous period. In July 1976, Mario Soares was
sworn in as head of a minority government based on
his Socialist Party which had 107 of the 263 seats
in the Assembly. With the economy heading further
into trouble, Soares apparently decided that the
socialism promised in the two-month-old Constitution should be shelved for the indefinite future.
He quickly announced a set of austerity measures,
including a 15 percent limit on wage increases (in
the face of an inflation rate expected to be at
least twice that high) and limits on government

spending.[25] More important was the announcement of
a plan to restrict the power of workers' representatives who were supposed to be on boards of all
companies with more than fifty employees.[26]

The quid pro quo on which Soares had his eye
had two parts. One was admission to the European
Economic Community (EEC) which he, like his Spanish
and Greek colleagues, believed to be the long-run
salvation of Portugal's democracy as well as its
economy. In early 1977, he made an eight-day trip
around Europe, soliciting support for Portuguese
membership. Soares' second goal was a large inflow
of foreign capital. Some had already come from the
EEC, which had reportedly loaned Portugal $1.2 bil-
lion during Soares' first nine months in office.[27]
But more important was the United States promise
to raise $1.5 billion from Western governments.
The idea was floated in late 1976 by Edwin Yeo,
Undersecretary of the Treasury for Monetary Affairs
and firm advocate of IMF discipline for "profligate"
governments.[28] Thus, it should have been no surprise when Yeo announced that the IMF would be
asked to manage the $1.5 billion.[29] In the mean-
time, the United States agreed to provide an emergency $300 million from the Treasury's Exchange
Stabilization Fund.

In line with its usual principle of not managing other people's money, the IMF refused to
directly participate in Yeo's scheme, but a second-
best strategy (from Yeo's point of view) was worked
out. The jumbo loan would "piggyback" on a Fund
program, i.e., it would be released only after Portugal had applied for and received an IMF loan with
stabilization measures attached. This led to
Soares' so-called "February measures".

The February measures, like those of the
previous year, were a combination of austerity and
structural change accelerating the return to
capitalism. The former included a 15 percent devaluation (compared to the IMF's original demand
of 20-25 percent) and an extension of the 15 percent wage ceiling. In addition, interest rates
were raised and government spending cuts were
promised. As an indication of the compromises the
Fund will accept, import controls were also introduced. The structural changes at this point were
the announcement that foreign investors would be
compensated for expropriated property within thirty
days and that 400 firms nationalized in 1975 would
be returned to their owners. In a step that was
reportedly designed to appease the left, social

security and unemployment benefits were extended,
and workers were given permission to take control
of "self-managed" factories if their former owners
did not counterclaim within two years. The government communique announcing the measures said they
were aimed to "save the national economy and defend
democracy."[30]

Whether they did either is open to question,
but they did pave the way for a $50 million IMF
standby. Since this amount was only equivalent to
a first tranche loan, the targets were only indicative. In its announcement of the standby, the
Fund described the program as follows:

> The Government's economic program, in support
> of which the present stand-by arrangement has
> been approved, is to reduce the balance of
> payments deficit by containing consumption
> and imports and to stimulate investment and
> exports. The former objective is to be
> achieved by limiting wage increases, by allow-
> ing prices to reflect cost developments, and
> by fiscal policy; the latter is to be sought
> through stepped-up public capital expenditure
> and measures to improve the financial position
> of enterprises, particularly changes in labor
> legislation designed to improve productivity.
> The depreciation of the escudo in February
> 1977 is an essential part of the program; by
> raising the domestic cost of imports and
> restoring the competitiveness of Portuguese
> exports, it can be expected to make a substan-
> tial contribution, in combination with the
> restraints placed on credit expansion, to the
> desired reduction in the balance of payments
> deficit.[31]

The February measures and the agreement with
the IMF produced the expected opposition within
Portugal. Labor and consumers protested,[32] the
Social Democrats demanded full debate on the
measures, and the Communist Party condemned them
as a way of making workers pay for Portugal's
economic problems. "Foreign loans are a garrotte
strangling the Portuguese economy," said PCP leader
Alvaro Cunbal. "The situation will not be cured by
loans, but by the joint effort of the people who
must be consulted."[33] On the other hand, they did
not produce the $1.5 billion. The United States
announced that its share was being postponed until
the 1978 fiscal budget (beginning in October),

while other governments indicated lack of enthusiasm. Speculation was that the United States and
others were trying to force Soares into a higher
tranche IMF loan that had more teeth.[34]

IMF Round II: 1977-78

By late 1977, it was clear that, far from getting better, Portugal's economic situation was
continuing to deteriorate. This can be seen by
looking back at Tables 3.1 to 3.3. The budget
deficit continued to increase as did inflation, but
the biggest problem remained the balance of payments deficit which, by the end of 1977, stood at
$1.5 billion or almost 10 percent of GNP. That
was what drove Portugal back to the IMF for the
second time.[35]

In what was perhaps an attempt to preempt the
Fund, Soares presented another set of measures to
the Assembly. Referred to this time as the "August
measures", these included a decision to float the
escudo, hoping it would depreciate at 1-2 percent
per month and thus cause less inflationary pressure
than had the one-shot 15 percent devaluation in
February. In addition, gasoline prices were raised,
the discount rate was increased by four points to
15.5 percent, and the 15 percent wage ceiling was
continued. In another move against the workers'
gains in the 1974-75 period, employers were now
given permission to fire "redundant" workers.[36]

With this as background, the IMF team arrived
in October, backed by special clout. The jumbo
loan--now cut to $750 million--had finally been
agreed to by 11 countries, but it had been clearly
stipulated that its release depended on Portugal
signing a letter of intent. The IMF loan itself
would be for another $50 million, so the whole
package would be worth $800 million. Looking
further ahead, it was clear that Portugal would
need much more money. The $800 million would not
even cover the balance of payments deficit, much
less finance development projects. The answer, as
a number of third world countries had discovered,
was the private capital markets, but there was little likelihood of Portugal obtaining private loans
before signing an agreement with the IMF.[37]

The Fund team arrived in a tough mood. They
wanted the deficit cut by one-third, to $800 mil-
lion from the then projected 1977 deficit of $1.2
billion. To accomplish this, they wanted deflation
to cut the growth rate from 6-7 percent to 4

percent, and a stiff devaluation to cut imports in
place of the February import controls.[38] Soares
agreed to introduce a budget aimed at heavy cuts
in public spending, plus large tax increases to cut
private consumption. At the same time, however, he
began a double campaign--to win support for austerity at home and to find allies abroad to pressure the IMF into greater leniency. Accordingly,
on the domestic side, he sought a four-party agreement on economic policy, including a "social pact"
with the unions (similar to the arrangements recently made in neighboring Spain).[39] Simultaneously, Soares stepped up an international campaign
begun earlier to get concessions from the Fund.
This time the models were Britain and especially
Italy which had both recently negotiated agreements with the IMF. The tactic was to play up
danger to Portugal's new democracy if austerity
measures were too stringent. Earlier in the year,
Soares had taken this campaign to IMF headquarters,
where he told managing director Johanes Witteveen
that "the Communists will be in the Azores" if
conditions were too tight.[40] Others in the government began to make similar statements. Finance
Minister Vitor Constancio, for instance, had the
following exchange with a reporter from a major
international financial journal:

Constancio: We only hope that the IMF, when
we negotiate with it, will allow
us sufficient flexibility to
avoid the social costs which
would lead to great political
problems.

Reporter: When you say great political problems, are you thinking of the
workers taking to the streets,
led by the Communist Party?

Constancio: Yes. If the social costs imposed
on us by the IMF are too high,
obviously that risk exists.[41]

In addition, an international media campaign
took shape, which some observers tied to the connections of the Socialist International of which
Soares is a vice-president. Editorials condemning
the IMF's hard line were published in Le Monde, the
Manchester Guardian, and even the New York Times.
The Times' fairy-tale style contribution ran as

follows:

> When Portugal's tired dictatorship gave way to
> a revolutionary spring four years ago, Mario
> Soares, the Socialist leader, held out a bold
> vision of the future. One of the poorest and
> least industrialized countries in Europe would
> establish democracy and join the Common Mar-
> ket, and thus transform itself into a modern
> and well-run society. Today, Mr. Soares is
> Prime Minister of a truly democratic Portugal
> but its progress is impeded. Political ad-
> vance is frustrated by economic constraint. . .
> To close the gap, Portugal has turned to the
> IMF, which insists on a credit squeeze, de-
> valuation, and restricted government spending.
> . . . It is appropriate medicine when the
> deficits result primarily from a consumer
> spending spree. But Portugal's situation is
> different. . . .[42]

Eventually Portugal did win some concessions, but
not before Soares' government was brought down in
a vote of confidence over the budget. All three
opposition parties (Social Democrats, Center Democrats, and Communists) voted against the Socialist
Party since none was willing to accept public con-
demnation for the resulting austerity as long as
Soares refused to share power. Ultimately he was
forced to form a coalition; his choice of partners
--the right-wing Center Democrats--revealed the
direction in which the Socialists were moving.
With Center Democratic support, Soares pushed the
budget through the Assembly. He also won some concessions from the IMF team, the most important
being the acceptance of a $1 billion deficit rather
than $800 million. It was reported that interest
rate and devaluation demands were softened as
well.[43] On this basis, a letter of intent was
signed, and it was approved by the Fund on June 12,
1978.
    What did Portugal finally agree to, and how
tough was the program in comparison to others
signed in Europe in the recent past? Table 3.4
provides some comparisons with the British and
Italian stabilization agreements. These comparisons among explicit targets indicate that Portugal
certainly got off easier than Britain. The credit
expansion targets were about the same, while both
the budget deficit and balance of payments targets
were more strict for Britain. In the case of

TABLE 3.4
Performance Criteria on IMF Loans to Britain, Italy, and Portugal

Country	Prev. 12 Months	Target	% Change*
Britain			
Budget deficit	—	—	—
Credit expansion	11.2 bil.	8.7 bil.	-22.3
Bal. of payments deficit	9 bil.	7.7 bil.	-14.5
	-2 bil.	-1 bil.	-50.0
Italy			
Budget deficit	-Lit 18,700 bil.	-Lit 16,450 bil.	-12.0
Credit expansion	27,218 bil.	30,000 bil.	+10.2
Bal. of payments deficit	-2,380 bil.	500 bil.	
Inflation**	22%	13%	-40.9
Portugal			
Budget deficit	-esc. 43 bil.	-esc. 45 bil.	+ 0.2
Credit expansion	167 bil.	142 bil.	-15.0
Bal. of payments deficit	-1.5 bil.	-1 bil.	-33.3

Source: Letters of Intent (Britain, Financial Times, December 16, 1976; Italy, Mondo Economico, April 23, 1977; Portugal, Diário de Noticias, May 19, 1978); IMF, International Financial Statistics.

* Nominal changes.
** Inflation index for scala mobile.

Italy, relevant evaluation would depend on the weight attached to different targets. In some respects Italy's conditions were tougher, in others Portugal's were. Further analysis would necessitate using the models mentioned earlier to compare implicit as well as explicit targets.

Concentrating only on the explicit targets for the moment, however, it is instructive to compare the severity of the programs with the seriousness of the economic problems the three countries faced. Presumably those with bigger problems would have more stringent programs if--as the Fund says--only technical economic criteria are used in setting targets. It is hard to reconcile that statement with the fact that although Britain's economic problems were far less serious than either Portugal's or Italy's, its austerity program was nevertheless the strictest. It would seem clear, then, that political factors did play an important role. Both Italy's Guilio Andreotti and Britain's James Callaghan had tried to gain concessions through leftist scare tactics as Soares did later; Andreotti was more successful because the Italian Communist Party posed a much more credible and immediate threat than the left wing of the British Labor Party. Portugal presumably lay in between.[44]

IMF Round III: 1978-79

Shortly after the letter of intent was finally signed and approved, the Socialist-Center Democrat coalition fell apart because the Center Democrats claimed that the Socialists were not moving fast enough in returning land and compensating owners of expropriated property. Faced with the prospect of elections, the parties agreed to the appointment of an independent, and Alfredo Nobre da Costa was named as Prime Minister. When he presented an austerity budget, however, he was voted down in the Assembly. The process was repeated with the appointment of another independent, law professor Carlos Mota Pinto. It thus fell to Mota Pinto to negotiate the renewal of the agreement with the IMF.

This new round of negotiations began in February 1979 and again involved a $50 million token loan. In spite of its small size, however, it was important because it was assumed at the time to be the key to the private capital markets. Disagreement arose almost immediately when the Portuguese team and the IMF stressed different aspects of Portugal's 1978 performance and thus different

proposals for 1979 targets. The government nego-
tiators concentrated on the balance of payments
outcome, pointing out that the actual results
($775 million deficit on current account) were much
better than the letter of intent target ($1 bil-
lion). Accordingly, they demanded a small refla-
tion of the economy in 1979. The Fund, on the
other hand, stressed the failure to meet the budget
deficit target (an overall deficit of escudos 68
billion compared to the letter of intent's escudos
45 billion), and termed the balance of payments
deficit and inflation as "excessive." Premature
relaxation of the stabilization effort would thus
be highly inadvisable in the opinion of the IMF
team.[45]
    The first round of talks thus ended in stale-
mate in March over several specific aspects of the
new stabilization program. First, there was disagreement over an appropriate balance of payments
target: while the Fund wanted an $800 million
limit, Portuguese officials, somewhat more pessi-
mistic about the effects of oil price increases,
pressed for $1 billion. Additional conflicts
emerged over the exchange rate and the interest
rate, credit allocations to the public vs. the private sector, and the reduction of restrictions on
trade.[46] In the meantime, the Mota Pinto government also ran into trouble in the Assembly, losing
a vote of confidence on its budget as the major
parties voted against a tax on workers' traditional
thirteenth month bonus.
    In April, informal conversations produced
"moderate optimism" about a new agreement.[47] The
necessity of such an arrangement, however, was soon
called into question when, at the end of May, the
Portuguese government reached a preliminary accord
with a syndicate of private banks for a $300 mil-
lion loan without an IMF "seal of approval." While
such approval had been made previously a sine qua
non condition for new loans, the banks apparently
changed their position in light of the improvement
in the balance of payments. As the vice-governor
of the Bank of Portugal said at the time, "A formal agreement with the IMF isn't as important as it
was a year ago."[48] The loan agreement was formally
signed in mid-July in spite of the political crisis
caused by the resignation of the Mota Pinto government (which had run into more opposition in the
Parliament). The banks' role in undermining the
Fund was further stressed several months later
when international bankers assured the government

that it would have access to the markets whether or not an agreement with the IMF was signed in 1980.[49]
    When no political coalition could be put together to govern the country, elections were reluctantly scheduled for December. They were won by the right-wing Democratic Alliance composed of Social Democrats, Christian Democrats, and Monarchists. The Alliance promised an acceleration of the steps initiated since 1976 to return to a free market economy (and to enter the EEC)--denationalization, encouragement of foreign investment, changes in labor laws, cuts in public expenditure. Although the new government's inclinations were closely in line with the recommendations of the IMF, it was decided not to enter into a formal agreement with the Fund--"a major political and economic gamble", in the words of one financial analyst, since the government would no longer use the IMF as "a convenient whipping boy for the austerity imposed on the population as a whole."[50]

5. THE POLITICAL ECONOMY OF STABILIZATION

    The question we now want to address is whether there are ways that are different (and preferable) to those followed by the Soares and successor governments for resolving economic disequilibria.[51] Three propositions are involved. First, there must be congruence between cause(s) and remedy(ies) of the disequilibria. Second, if the causes are primarily structural, stabilization must be part of a long-term strategy to overcome the structural problems. Third, the type of long-term strategy must be selected in light of its effects on income distribution as well as on the growth prospects of the economy.
    That the cause of a disequilibrium should be taken into consideration in determining a remedy might appear to be so obvious as not to require discussion. Yet, the IMF has generally tended to prescribe remedies relating to the elimination of excess demand, in spite of indications that this was not always the cause of disequilibrium.[52] More specifically, by ignoring the possibility that inflation and balance of payments deficits might be due to structural causes, the Fund dismissed solutions quite different from those appropriate for "demand pull" or even "cost push" disequilibria.[53]
    The latter is a debate with a long tradition in the Latin American context, especially with

respect to inflation, between the so-called "mone-
tarists" and "structuralists." Indeed, many of
the discussions held with the IMF (which until
recently was much more active in Latin America than
in Europe) have been pursued within this framework.[54] Although not accepting all the implications of the structuralists' arguments, we do
strongly endorse their initial point: attempting
to resolve disequilibria merely by dampening demand
may provide a temporary solution but not a permanent one, as it will be attacking the symptoms
rather than the root causes. Once the immediate
disequilibria (inflation and balance of payments
deficits) have disappeared, expansion will be allowed again and the disequilibria will quickly
return. In the current Portuguese case, it might
be observed, only one aspect of the disequilibria
(balance of payments) was controlled via deflation;
inflation continued almost as strong as before.

Let us take one of the most obvious examples
of a structural problem contributing to inflation
and the balance of payments deficit in Portugal--
the production of food. For years Portugal--again
like many Latin American countries--neglected its
agricultural sector in favor of fast industrial
growth. The result was rapidly rising prices for
food and a growing need to rely on imports. For
example, between 1967 and 1973 (i.e., prior to the
revolution), wholesale food prices in Lisbon increased by 30.1 percent compared with only 22.9
percent for manufactured goods.[55] Likewise, Portugal's food deficit (food exports minus imports)
began in 1970 and rose to almost $100 million by
1973; food imports that year represented about 14
percent of total imports.[56] Now, it is certainly
possible to resolve the inflationary and balance of
payments effects of the food problem by cutting
demand; people will eat less and the problem will
temporarily disappear.[57] However, either the
clamp on demand will have to be maintained perma-
nently--which is more difficult in a democracy than
under the dictatorship that Portugal previously
experienced--or the disequilibrium will return as
soon as the clamp is released. The only way to
permanently resolve problems deriving from food
shortages is to increase the production of food.[58]
There are, of course, various theories as to how
food production should be stimulated, but to deny
that such considerations are relevant is to make
economic analysis useless for policy making.

Other examples of structural problems leading

to economic disequilibria in Portugal come from the
end of the Portuguese empire in Africa as it en-
tailed the return of the troops and settlers, the
loss of markets, and the loss of sources of cheap
raw materials. In turn, these led to increased
unemployment and inflationary pressures, lower export revenues than would otherwise have been the
case, and higher import costs. The problems here
are much more varied than in the food example, but
they again demand long-run structural solutions,
including the creation of new sources of employment, the restructuring of industry, the search for
new markets, and the search for alternative sources
of supply or the switch to substitutes. Once more,
recession can temporarily contain these problems
(except unemployment), but it can provide no lasting solution.

It should be pointed out that the IMF has
taken at least two positive steps in the last few
years with respect to stabilization. On the one
hand, it has changed its expectation that one-year
adjustment programs should be the norm and introduced the possibility of longer periods of adjustment through the Extended Fund Program and the
Witteveen Facility. On the other hand, as of March
1979, it openly acknowledged the fact that cause
and remedy should be related (presumably implying
that such was not the case previously). In a new
set of guidelines with respect to conditionality in
stabilization programs, the Executive Board of the
Fund directed its staff to "pay due regard to the
domestic social and political objectives, the economic priorities, and the circumstances of members,
including the causes of their balance of payments
problems."[59] The more general problem, however--
the stress on the separation of "stabilization" and
"development"--remains. The possibility that lasting stabilization can only be rooted in longer-term
development is either not accepted by the IMF or is
thought to be irrelevant given its mandate to deal
with short-term problems. "We are not a development agency" is the Fund's answer to such
criticisms.[60]

Nevertheless, it is clear that there is an
implicit development strategy behind the IMF's
stabilization policies. On the one hand, it emphasizes private enterprise and especially foreign
capital. On the other hand, it stresses an open
economy and export promotion. The dismantling of
controls and the lowering of real wages are both
essential parts of this model which appears to have

been largely shared by the post-1975 Portuguese
governments. Whether this strategy can resolve
Portugal's growth and employment problems is certainly debatable; the accompanying negative redistribution of income is much clearer.[61]
        If such a redistribution is considered unac-
ceptable--either for ethical reasons or for fear of
its political consequences--if the working class,
and especially the weakest among the workers, are
not to be asked to pay the vast majority of the
costs, then stabilization must be embedded in a
different kind of development model. Even if one
does not believe that a transition to socialism was
a viable option for Portugal in 1974-75,[62] the alternative was not necessarily laissez-faire capitalism. On the contrary, the key element of any alternative which protects workers' incomes, and at the
same time generates high enough growth rates to
guarantee full employment, must assign a very strong
economic role to the state.
        Within the European context, both the British
and the Italians have been discussing possible ways
to accomplish such goals without running into
balance of payments constraints. Because the emphasis is on development, with stabilization as an
integral part of the development process, discussion has focused not on the IMF's deflation/devalu-
ation duo but on the relative merits of devaluation
vs. import controls.[63] At the academic level, the
British debate has been between groups of Cambridge
and Oxford economists, but both groups have acted
as advisors to political factions as well.
        Both sides agree that traditional government
policy, followed by Labor and Tory governments
alike, has exacerbated the structural decline of
British industry, thus endangering the economy as
a whole. The conclusion of the Cambridge group is
that the economy needs some breathing space for
investment and the restructuring of industry in
order to regain its competitive position (the
infant, or rather ancient, industry argument). The
basic mechanism would be stimulation of import
substitution by the private sector; references are
made to Germany, the United States, and other
countries that imposed import restrictions to
strengthen their then non-competitive industries,
later to emerge as exporters. Given unemployment
and unused capacity, it is argued that there would
be an immediate increase in production to replace
the banned imports; new investment would then follow. The decreased volume (and value) of imports,

even with a constant flow of exports, would eliminate the negative trade balance, and the higher
growth rate would permit an increase in real wages
without causing inflation. Cambridge arguments
against devaluation are deteriorating terms of
trade, inflationary effects, regressive redistribution of income (via inflation producing a decline
in real wages accompanied by an increase in profits), and the slow nature and uncertainty of devaluation. These problems are exacerbated by the very
large nominal devaluation needed to significantly
improve a country's competitive position.[64]

The Oxford economists make two basic kinds of
attacks on the Cambridge strategy. First, they
claim that, with the exception of deteriorating
terms of trade, all the negative effects accruing
through devaluation would also be present with
import controls. The effects of import controls
would also be delayed by the necessity to create a
bureaucracy. The inflationary effects would occur
in both models, as would regressive redistribution
(via the increase in profits needed to induce investment). Second, the Oxford group attacks the
idea of controls per se, as these are said to lead
to inefficiency, corruption, and monopoly among
other vices. In short, market mechanisms are seen
as a preferable way to bring about growth.[65]

The most precise form of the debate derives
from the simulations of the Cambridge Economic
Policy Group based on their model of the British
economy.[66] Comparisons are made of the orthodox
strategy (i.e., avoiding balance of payments constraints through deflation), devaluation, and
import controls. Various assumptions about world
trade and prices, balance of payments targets, public expenditure and taxation, and nominal wage
settlements are held constant among the three strategies with differences emerging in terms of growth
rates, unemployment, inflation, and income distribution. Table 3.5 shows the results of such a
simulation.

In the Italian case,[67] and among a third group
of British economists,[68] a more radical version of
the imports controls strategy is being discussed.
Believing as they do that the private sector cannot
be relied on to undertake investment in the way
necessary to sustain full employment, these economists and their political counterparts therefore
conclude that the state must assume the dominant
role in the accumulation process. This would involve state ownership of key industries, a planning

process for deciding the allocation of resources,
as well as the actual investment itself. In addition to providing for a rapid growth rate, a
further advantage of state intervention is in terms
of income distribution since a smaller share of the
surplus would be diverted to capitalist consumption.
Such a system is obviously not equivalent to socialism, but could have been a preferable alternative
to the Soares/IMF policies in Portugal after 1975.

The British experience, and discussions related to that experience, are relevant for Portugal
in spite of the fact that Portugal's economy is
still much more dynamic than Britain's. That is,
it is policies such as Portugal has adopted over
the past five years--stabilization based on deflation while moving back toward private enterprise--
that are largely responsible for the stagnation of
the British economy. The resulting stop-go growth
pattern led to the vicious circle of low investment,
failure to introduce new technology, lack of competitiveness, low demand, higher unit costs, lower
profits, and thus low investment. Italy's situation is even more similar to that of Portugal, and
there the deflation/devaluation path has also led
to stop-go and lower growth than necessary to
achieve and maintain full employment. In addition,
the British and Italian experience as lesser
developed countries within the EEC might be relevant for study in Portugal.

6. CONCLUSIONS

To conclude, we will summarize the main points
of the paper and then return to the question of the
role of the IMF.

(1) The Portuguese governments of 1974-75
wanted to increase the level of economic development and change the distribution of income, wealth,
and power. They tried to accomplish these goals
through short-term economic policies (increasing
wages, freezing prices, and increasing public expenditures) and structural change (nationalization
and worker participation as part of a transition
to socialism).

(2) The results of these actions, plus various
external problems (oil price increases, international recession, end of empire), led to serious
disequilibria in the economy (especially inflation
and balance of payments deficits).

TABLE 3.5
Projected Outcomes for Different Development Strategies in British Economy,
1980-90

	Orthodox	Devaluation*	Imp. Cont.**
GDP growth (1973=100)			
1980	108	111	114
1985	116	133	139
1990	116	154	167
Unemployment (millions)			
1980	1.8	1.5	1.3
1985	2.5	1.5	1.0
1990	4.6	1.4	0.5
Avg. real earnings, post-tax (1973=100)			
1980	101	102	101
1985	113	109	119
1990	124	119	144
Inflation			
1980	10.6%	11.7%	10.6%
1985	5.0	6.2	3.9
1990	6.4	10.2	4.1

Income distribution (property &
entrepreneurial income/wages and
salaries)

1980	67.8%	62.9%	62.4%
1985	57.4	70.7	56.2
1990	63.6	84.5	53.7

Source: Calculated from F. Cripps, M. Fetherstone, and T. Ward, "The Effects of Different Strategies for the UK Economy," Economic Policy Review, 4 (March 1978), pp. 5-21 and Appendix.

* Four percent improvement in cost competitiveness per year.
** Quotes on manufactured imports to meet growth targets.

(3) The Portuguese governments of 1976-79 saw
their basic task as eliminating the disequilibria
via orthodox stabilization measures (reducing
spending and the money supply, cutting wages) and
moving toward greater reliance on the private
sector.

(4) The Soares policies at least temporarily
dampened one aspect of the disequilibria (balance
of payments deficit), but at the cost of recession
and regressive redistribution of income and wealth.

(5) There are other methods of approaching
stabilization that would have been more appropriate,
given the causes of disequilibrium in Portugal.
Most importantly, stabilization should have been
seen as part of a long-run development strategy
aimed at resolving structural obstacles to growth.
In order to promote rapid growth, while avoiding
negative redistribution, such a strategy would have
had to reserve a strong role for the state while
taking unorthodox measures to avoid balance of payments constraints.

What was the IMF's role in the choice of policies in Portugal? Three points are important to
make. First, the Portuguese policies closely
paralleled those normally advocated by the Fund,
both in their short-term and long-term aspects.
Deflation, an open economy, and private enterprise
are key to all Fund programs. Second, this does
not mean that such decisions were "imposed" by the
IMF on an unwilling Portuguese government. On the
contrary, there is no indication that the Soares
and successor governments wanted to take an unorthodox route. Third, the real role of the IMF was
to reinforce (and probably exacerbate) existing
inclinations toward dismantling structural reforms
and forcing workers to pay the main cost of stabilization. Furthermore, such inclinations were
legitimized by the IMF, both domestically and
internationally. Through use of their image as an
apolitical group of experts, the Fund gave pro-
foundly political decisions a technical veneer and
eulogized them as "sound economic policy."

NOTES

1. Articles of Agreement of the International
Monetary Fund, IMF, Washington, DC, 1945. See
also the discussion in J. Keith Horsefield, editor,
The International Monetary Fund, 1945-65, IMF,

Washington, DC, 1969, Vol. II, Chapter 2.

2. IMF, Annual Report, 1948. See also Horsefield.

3. For a discussion of the role of the IMF and its relationship to other funding agencies, see B. Stallings, "Peru and the U.S. Banks: The Privatization of International Finance," in R. Fagen, ed., Capitalism and the State in U.S.-Latin American Relations, Stanford University Press, 1979, pp. 217-53.

4. Interviews with IMF officials.

5. See A. Mateus, "Growth, Inflation, and External Equilibrium: The Case of Portugal," paper delivered at Committee on Atlantic Studies Conference on "Inflation and Political Change," Berlin, September 1978. In trying to determine the adequacy of the model as a reflection of IMF thinking, I consulted a long-time Fund advisor who deemed it "very accurate"; Fund officials declined comment.

6. On different views in different divisions of the IMF, see B. Stallings, "The IMF in Europe: Inflation Fighting in Britain, Italy, and Portugal," in L. Lindberg, ed., Inflation and Political Change, Pergamon Press, forthcoming.

7. People associated with the IMF confirm the use of devaluation as a way of cutting wages. See E.V.R. Fitzgerald, "The Limitations of State Capitalism as a Model of Economic Development: Peru 1968-78," in A. Lowenthal and C. McClintock, eds., The Peruvian Experiment Reconsidered, Princeton University Press, forthcoming, footnote 23.

8. Interviews with IMF officials.

9. See further discussion below.

10. Calculated from OECD, Economic Surveys: Portugal, December 1977, pp. 57-58.

11. L.L. Vasconcelos and C. Garrido, "Structural Changes and Development Trends in Portugal Since 1974," September 1977, mimeo, p. 19.

12. OECD, p. 57.

13. Vasconcelos and Garrido, pp. 15-17.

14. See A.R. Santos, "Desenvolvimento monopolista em Portugal, 1968-73," Analise Social, #49 (1977) and B. Martins, Sociedades e grupos em Portugal, Lisbon, 1973.

15. OECD, pp. 43,58.

16. See interview with Walter Marques, member of Board of Directors of Bank of Portugal, in Euromoney, March 1978, pp. 22-23.

17. Reserves in 1973 were equal to $2.839 billion, of which almost half was gold. At market prices, of course, the reserves would be worth

132

much more. See IMF, International Financial Statistics, March 1979.
  18. Calculated from OECD, p. 54. See also, "Survey on Portugal," The Economist, May 28, 1977, p. 22.
  19. OECD, Main Economic Indicators, January 1975.
  20. For an excellent analysis of the political aspects of the Portuguese revolution, see K. Maxwell, "The Hidden Revolution in Portugal" and "Portugal under Pressure," New York Review of Books, XXII, 6 (April 7, 1975) pp. 29-35 and XXII, 9 (May 29, 1975) pp. 20-30 respectively. See also Chapter 1 of this book by T. Bruneau.
  21. Calculated from OECD, Portugal, 1977, pp. 15,59.
  22. Ibid., p. 11.
  23. IMF, International Financial Statistics, March 1979. For a more detailed review of economic policies and consequences after 1974, see Chapter 2 of this book by P. Krugman and J. B. de Macedo.
  24. Vasconcelos and Garrido, pp. 25-32.
  25. The Economist, September 18, 1976.
  26. Ibid., July 31, 1976.
  27. Observer News Service, April 20, 1977.
  28. Yeo and then Treasury Secretary William Simon had previously designed a scheme to force the U.K. to go to the IMF. See the three-part series in Sunday Times (London), May 14, May 21, and May 28, 1978. IMF officials confirm the general accuracy of these articles though saying they "overstress the American role a bit."
  29. Financial Times, November 25, 1976.
  30. Ibid., February 26, 1977 and The Economist, March 5, 1977.
  31. IMF Survey, May 2, 1977. Since this was a first tranche loan, no letter of intent was required.
  32. Financial Times, February 24, 1977 and March 9, 1977; Times (London), March 2, 1977.
  33. Financial Times, March 3, 1977.
  34. Financial Times, February 16, 1977 and February 24, 1977.
  35. In reality, Portugal still had plenty of reserves to cover the balance of payments deficit, but by that time the reserves consisted almost entirely of gold which had special symbolic import in Portugal. Selling off the country's gold supply would thus have dangerous political consequences for a government which did so.
  36. The Economist, September 3, 1977.

37. Peru, under similar straits in mid-1976, had gone directly to the banks for balance of payments support, rather than dealing with the IMF. The resulting problems and criticism from within the banking world itself made another such venture highly unlikely. See Stallings, "Peru and the U.S. Banks."

38. The Economist, November 19, 1977.

39. Ibid., September 3, 1977 and November 19, 1977.

40. Interviews with IMF officials.

41. Euromoney, March 1978, p. 20. The article was published under the melodramatic title of "Across the Tagus, Communism Waits."

42. New York Times, March 25, 1978.

43. Le Monde, May 6, 1978.

44. See Stallings, "The IMF in Europe."

45. Interviews with Portuguese economic officials.

46. Ibid. See also Financial Times, March 7, 1979.

47. See press conference by Bank of Portugal Governor Jose Silva Lopes on returning from meetings with the IMF in Washington in Expresso, April 21, 1979.

48. Wall Street Journal, May 29, 1979.

49. Financial Times, October 26, 1979.

50. Ibid., January 29, 1980.

51. The other question inherent in the previous discussion--whether there are alternative (and preferable) ways to redistribute--must be left for another occasion. See S.-C. Kolm, La transition socialiste, Cerf, Paris, 1977.

52. The IMF is not alone in denying a necessary relationship between cause and remedy. In Chapter 2 of this book, for instance, P. Krugman and J.B. de Macedo say, "The attempt to use the cause of disequilibrium to determine the remedy is a mistake. . . . Whatever the cause of disequilibrium, conventional macroeconomic analysis i.e. demand cutting can still be used to determine the way back to equilibrium."

53. An interesting example is found in the Portuguese case itself. Although IMF's own economists (together with those of the OECD) term the current Portuguese inflation profits-led, cutting public expenditure (and wages) is still seen as the proper remedy.

54. For a discussion of the IMF in Latin America and some of these issues, see R. Thorp and L. Whitehead, eds., Inflation and Stabilization

in Latin America, Macmillan, London, 1979. An early
statement of the monetarist-structuralist debate is
found in A. Hirschman, ed., Latin American Issues:
Essays and Answers, Twentieth Century Fund, New
York, 1961 (articles by Campos, Felix, and Grun-
wald).

55. Calculated from OECD, Portugal, 1977, p.
48.

56. Ibid., p. 54.

57. Perhaps the most striking example is post-
Allende Chile. There the government congratulated
itself on finally becoming a net exporter of meat
and milk after decades as an importer. The fact
that real wages had dropped so drastically that
demand for such products almost disappeared was not
considered relevant.

58. On the general question of food production
and economic disequilibrium, see M. Kalecki, Essays
on Developing Economies, Harvester Press, 1976,
Chapters 5 and 7. Kalecki makes this factor a
central part of his model.

59. IMF Survey, March 19, 1979 (emphasis
added).

60. UNCTAD has made similar arguments with
respect to third world countries. See The Balance
of Payments Adjustment Process in Developing Countries: Report to the Group of 24, UNDP/UNCTAD Project INT/75/015, January 1979.

61. Before the revolution, Portugal had the
second highest level of inequality in the OECD
world. In 1970, only Greece had a lower share of
national income going to labor than did Portugal.
The range was from Greece's 33 percent to the
United States' 69 percent, with Portugal at 47 percent. The Portuguese figure rose to a high of 63
percent in 1975 before beginning to fall again.
Calculated from OECD, National Account Statistics
of OECD Countries, 1960-77, Vol. II, Paris, 1979.

62. A number of factors led to doubts about
the possibility of a transition to socialism in the
mid-1970s. In external terms, Portugal would have
required strong economic backing from the Soviet
Union to offset its geographical and historical
proximity to the NATO countries. There is no indication that Moscow was willing to provide such
help; another Cuba was not desired. In domestic
terms, the low level of economic development and
the low level of political consciousness and organization also constituted obstacles to a type of
socialism that did not merely replicate that of
Eastern Europe.

63. The IMF alternative of deflation or devaluation is more restricted than it appears. As
will be seen below, devaluation can be a strategy
for growth; in the IMF context, however, it was
basically a means of cutting wages. Thus deflation
is the only real option.
64. This argument is presented by the Cambridge
Economic Policy Group in various issues of their
yearly publication Economic Policy Review. See also
the formal presentation of the model in F. Cripps
and W. Godley, "A Formal Analysis of the Cambridge
Economic Policy Group Model," Economica, November
1976.
65. See W.M. Corden et al., Import Controls
vs. Devaluation and Britain's Economic Prospects,
Trade Policy Research Center, Guest Paper No. 2,
1975.
66. For general critiques of the CEPG model,
not limited to the import controls controversy, see
K. Brunner and A. Meltzer, eds., Public Policies in
Open Economies, North-Holland, Amsterdam, 1978
(suppl. series to Journal of Monetary Economics,
No. 9). Articles by Blinder, Hall, Frenkel, and
Russell & Wakeman discuss different aspects of the
model.
67. See G. de Vivo and M. Pivetti, "International Integration and the Balance of Payments Constraint: The Case of Italy," Cambridge Journal of
Economics, IV, 1 (March 1980), pp. 1-22.
68. See, for example, M. Ellman et al.,
Britain's Economic Crisis, Spokesman Pamphlet No.
44, 1974.

COMMENT

Patrick de Fontenay

Rather than to attempt to set the record
straight and to correct all the errors of fact and
interpretation in Ms. Stallings' paper, my comments
will focus on her conclusions on the role of the
IMF (the Fund), with special reference to Portugal.
Ms. Stallings' main criticisms of stabilization programs supported by the Fund's financial
assistance are (i) that they are inadequate to
solve the problems of a country like Portugal, and
(ii) that they are biased in favor of reliance on
free market forces, as opposed to controls. On the
first point, she argues that Portugal's balance of
payments problems were structural in nature, and
therefore that investment and planning, not deflation were the appropriate remedy.
Properly speaking, "structural" is of a
long-term nature and does not refer to factors on
which the country has no control like the rise in
energy prices or the world recession, which both
contributed to the worsening of Portugal's balance
of payments deficit. The Fund provides financial
assistance with mild conditionality to member
countries that experience deficits arising out of
export shortfalls that are regarded as both
temporary and largely beyond the control of the
member. Portugal availed itself of this "com-
pensatory financing facility". The "oil facilities"
of 1974 and 1975, with their limited conditionality, were also set up to allow the financing of
the payments deficits resulting from the oil price
rise in 1973-74 and to avoid reinforcing the
recessionary tendencies in the world economy.
Portugal availed itself also of these facilities.
But except for these special cases, the Fund has
taken the view that a country making use of the
Fund's resources must do so in the framework of an

economic policy program aimed at improving its external payments position. Even that part of the balance of payments deficit resulting from unfavorable developments, like the severance of ties between Portugal and its overseas territories, the loss of employment opportunities for Portuguese workers in Europe, or the disorganization of Portuguese agriculture, could not be financed indefinitely.

The Fund has at the same time recognized that the correction of structural maladjustments in the economy or of conditions impeding export growth takes time, and the duration of programs supported by the Fund has been lengthening in recent years, particularly, although not exclusively, under the "extended Fund facility" which can cover periods up to three years. And repayment periods may now extend to seven years for the supplementary financing facility and ten years for the extended Fund facility. The main reason why Portugal has not yet made use of these facilities is that, contrary to what Ms. Stallings asserts, the balance of payments deficits in 1976 and 1977 were only partly due to structural factors. Overspending--resulting from dramatic increases in real wages and from larger budget deficits--, and inappropriate exchange rate and interest rate policies, which contributed to the speculative stockpiling of finished and intermediate goods and of raw materials, were the main causes of the surge in the volume of imports (averaging more than 15 percent in both years), and of the hemorrhage of official reserves. Until these serious problems had been dealt with, it was hardly possible to consider the implementation of a medium-term program.

Ms. Stallings, like some others in Portugal and elsewhere, criticizes the impact of the Fund programs (mainly through credit restraint) on investment. There is no gainsaying the importance of investment for a developing country like Portugal, but the size of an investment program is limited by the level of domestic savings and by the amount of the external financing available. A balance of payments deficit of the size of that recorded in 1977 by Portugal, even if it had resulted from a massive investment effort, which certainly was not the case, could not be sustained very long as it would quickly exhaust the financing available from the Fund or other sources. In practice, the maintenance of a satisfactory level of investment will therefore depend on the success

of economic policies in "making room" for the desired investment by curbing private and public consumption and in reducing that part of the balance
of payments deficit which is not related to the
investment effort. Another limitation on investment is the absorptive capacity of the country in
terms of its ability to plan, evaluate and implement investment programs that are economically
viable. Incidentally, direct foreign investment,
which Ms. Stallings dislikes so much, is not subject to these constraints.

Whether a decline in output (or marked decel-
eration) can be avoided during a stabilization
program will depend mainly on (i) the desired speed
of adjustment, (ii) the severity of the problem,
and (iii) the degree of success in "expenditure
switching policies." The first point is related to
the next one: if a country defers taking corrective
action--whether by itself or within the framework of
a Fund program--until its difficulties have become
acute, then it may be hard to avoid more severe
measures than would have been necessary for adjustment at an earlier date. Developing countries have
often complained that the adjustment required by
Fund programs is too abrupt,[1] but it is by no means
certain that a gradual approach to taking corrective
measures is politically easier, because of the
persistence it requires, than a bold decisive action
which may be more easily acceptable in the context
of an exchange crisis or other serious difficulty.
The last point refers to the role of the exchange
rate in stimulating production of exports and
import substitutes, and to the crucial importance
of real wage flexibility.

The policies introduced by the Portuguese
authorities, and supported by the 1978 stand-by
arrangement with the Fund, had a major role in
halving the $1.5 billion deficit in the current
account of the balance of payments recorded in 1977.
Meanwhile real GDP growth decelerated modestly from
5 per cent in 1977 to 3 per cent in 1978 (and
probably also in 1979). Admittedly, a 3 per cent
growth rate is insufficient given Portugal's
development needs but in view of the magnitude of
the external adjustment achieved and the slow
growth in Portugal's trading partners, it is not an
inconsiderable achievement. Many other hard-
pressed countries would no doubt have been prepared
to pay such a price in terms of output forgone for
a balance of payments adjustment of such a significant magnitude. The realistic exchange rate and

interest rate policies pursued contributed to a
rapid expansion of exports, as well as to substantial inflows of workers' remittances. As incentives for speculative stockbuilding were eliminated,
imports actually declined. The overall balance of
payments improved even more than the current account
as the higher interest rates and the crawling peg
system discouraged speculative capital outflows. It
is true that only a small temporary dip in the rate
of inflation was achieved. The Fund's experience
has been generally that the inflation problem is
more intractable than balance of payments disequilibria.

Ms. Stallings charges that all Fund stabilization programs have to offer is a combination of
deflation and devaluation, the burden of which
falls inevitably on the workers in the form of
higher unemployment, lower real wages, or both.
She attributes this singlemindedness to the Fund's
preference for relying on free market forces as
opposed to controls and planning which she favors.
It must be made clear, however, that the Fund,
whose membership of 139 countries runs the gamut
from market oriented countries to centrally planned
economies, does not attempt to change the basic
character or organization of a member's economy.
In the words of the Fund's former General Counsel,"
. . . the degree to which the economy is under
government ownership or control is accepted as
part of the framework within which a program of
adjustment must be made to fit. Similarly, the
social objectives or priorities of a member are
accepted as beyond negotiation, subject to the
proviso that the policies to promote them will
permit the member to achieve a sustainable balance
of payments position. In short, the Fund does not
seek to modify the political or social policies of
a member. The character of the Fund is determined
by its technical tasks, the principle of universal
membership, and the uniform treatment of all
members."[1]

What may give the impression that the Fund
represents "international capitalist forces" is the
Fund's insistence that solutions to balance of
payments problems should not be sought in restrictions on trade and payments. This insistence is
simply a recognition that policies supported by
the Fund's financial assistance must be consistent
with the purposes of the Fund as stated in the
first of the Articles of Agreement of the IMF. By
shortening the duration and lessening the extent

of disequilibrium in the payments balances of
members, the Fund is expected to reduce the incentive for discriminatory exchange and payments
practices, in order to facilitate the expansion
and balanced growth of international trade. It is
to contribute thereby to the development of the
productive resources and the promotion of high
levels of employment and real wages of all member
countries alike. Restrictions are likely to intensify and not correct the distortions that give
rise to the need for external adjustment, and thus
to provide at best only a temporary improvement in
the external payments position, while creating
possible harm for other countries in the process.

The other reason for Ms. Stallings' characteri-
zation of Fund supported programs is probably
related to the numerous occasions on which that
institution has drawn attention to the structural
effects of interferences with the price mechanism
introduced for otherwise respectable and well-
intentioned purposes. For example, it is now
widely recognized that rent controls affect construction adversely and create or aggravate
housing shortages; that outright bans on lay-offs
discourage new hirings; that high minimum wage
rates tend to aggravate unemployment particularly
for youths; that attempts artificially to keep down
the price of staples will serve as disincentives to
the production of just these items.

It is an illusion to believe that controls
could have prevented for long a decline in the real
wages of Portuguese workers. As Ms. Stallings
notes, for a while the purchasing power of the
very large increases in nominal wage rates granted
in 1974-75 was artificially protected through
price controls, an overvalued exchange rate which
kept down the price of imports, and subsidies.
This could not be kept up very long, however,
because of the effects of these measures on the
deficits of both the government budget and the
balance of payments. Soon, it became obvious that
the level of real wage rates was not compatible
with both full employment and a sustainable
balance of payments deficit and that the decline in
productivity, the loss in terms of trade (resulting
in part from the rise in oil prices) and the influx
of refugees from the former overseas territories
argued for a decline, not a rise, in real wage
rates. Such a decline would have taken place re-
gardless of the Government's wage policy. It is
also hazardous to draw conclusions on a country's

income distribution from the behavior of wage rates.
When a large percentage of the labor force is
unemployed, as in Portugal, an increase in wages
widens the gap between the living standards of
those who have employment and those who have not.
And it is always possible for a government to aim
at income redistribution through taxes and transfers without directly changing the level or
structure of wage rates.

Finally, it must be recognized on this issue
of reliance on controls, that the opening of the
Portuguese economy to the outside in order to
benefit from the international division of labor
and the flow of foreign investment was not imposed
by the Fund. It stemmed from the decision of the
Portuguese people through its democratically
elected representatives to seek membership in the
European Economic Community and to participate in
a common market with the other members of the EEC.
It is likely that this decision, in turn, reflected
the historical and geographical orientation of
Portugal's toward the outside.

NOTES

1. See, for example, the statement delivered
at the 34th Annual Meeting of the IMF by Eric O.
Bell, Jamaica's Minister of Finance and Planning,
in IMF Survey, October 15, 1979, p. 308.

2. Joseph Gold, "Financial Assistance by the
International Monetary Fund: Law and Practice,"
IMF Pamphlet No. 27, Washington, D.C., 1979, p. 20.

COMMENT

The Political Economy of Stabilization

Pentti J.K. Kouri

Barbara Stallings' paper attacks conventional macroeconomic policies on many fronts and is particularly critical of the "sound economic policies" that she associates specifically with the International Monetary Fund (IMF). These policies consist typically of "deflation and devaluation" and are aimed at reducing or eliminating a deficit in the balance of payments. She argues that such "conventional" policies fail to take into account the root causes of macroeconomic disequilibria, and only suppress the symptoms of more fundamental problems without providing a lasting cure. As she puts it in discussing Portugal's food problem, "whilst it is possible to resolve the inflationary and balance of payments effects of the food problem by cutting demand . . . either the clamp on demand has to be maintained indefinitely . . . or the disequilibrium will return as the clamp is released."

Stallings also criticizes the IMF for advocating and promoting trade and payments liberalization; for emphasizing private enterprise and foreign capital and for stressing an open economy and export promotion. Such free market ideology inhibits, in her view, consideration of "unorthodox policies", such as import controls, which might be more effective than devaluation in eliminating the balance of payments constraint on growth.

Stallings argues further that stabilization strategy should be selected "in light of its effects on incomes distribution as well as the growth prospects of the economy" and criticizes IMF policies for putting the burden of adjustment on the working class. She calls for stabilization policy that is "embedded in a different kind of development model". She is not, however, very clear about what this alternative model is, beyond stating that "the key

element of any alternative which protects workers'
incomes, and at the same time generates high enough
growth rates to guarantee full employment, must
assign a very strong economic role to the state"
. . while taking "unorthodox measures to avoid
balance of payments constraints."

It is not an easy task to discuss all of these
arguments in one brief comment but I shall nevertheless try to do so from the perspective of what
Barbara Stallings probably would call orthodox
economics.

CAUSES AND REMEDIES

A central theme in Stallings' paper is the
argument that stabilization policy should take into
account the root causes of disequilibria. She seems
to use the word "cause" in at least two different
meanings. On the one hand, it seems to refer to
some historical disturbance, or disturbances, that
shocked the economy away from equilibrium, such as
exogenous decline in agricultural output, which
Stallings claims to be important in the Portuguese
context. On the other hand, "root cause" appears
to refer to something -- not clearly explained --
which makes the attainment of equilibrium impossible
by means of aggregate demand and exchange rate policies. Thus, in discussing Portugal's food problem,
Stallings appears to argue that decline in domestic
food supply led to a structural current account
deficit which can be suppressed but not eliminated
by clamping down on aggregate demand. As she puts
it, -- to repeat --; "either the clamp on demand
will have to be maintained permanently . . . or the
disequilibrium will return as soon as the clamp is
released." The only solution, she argues, is to
increase the production of food. She does not,
however, explain how that is to be done, beyond
stating that "there are . . . various theories as
to how food production should be stimulated." Apparently, price incentive is not important in any
of these theories, since there is no discussion in
the paper of agricultural prices, or of the effects
of exchange rate policy on agricultural production
and trade.

Stallings takes it as self-evident that government should deal with each sector specific problem,
without giving any indication as to what government
should, or could, do. Presumably she has in mind
subsidies, trade restrictions and other, more direct
forms of government intervention.

Sector specific policies do have political appeal since they appear to provide a concrete solution to a concrete problem. A good example is the
response to the oil crisis. Energy policy has been
seen as the solution of the problem in all countries
that have been hit by the increase in the relative
price of imported oil. Yet, many of the policies
that have been advocated, and in some cases, implemented under the umbrella of energy policy, introduce
economic waste, threaten the environment, and often
make no contribution to the solution of the narrowly
defined energy problem either.
Often such policies are introduced with the
purpose of reducing future energy shortage, measured
as the difference between demand and supply at an
exogenously given price: they attempt to restore
equilibrium at this price by shifting supply and
demand schedules. The approach of an economist is
in contrast to say that there cannot be a "shortage"
of an individual commodity, only general scarcity
of resources and lack of general purchasing power by
some groups in society. Efficient utilization of
scarce resources requires that prices of individual
commodities reflect their relative scarcity. In
this way resources will be reallocated over a period
of time to their most valuable use. Distribution of
income is in turn best handled by income transfers
rather than by arbitrary price controls which
create shortages and distortions in resource
allocation.
Consider in more detail the problem of adjusting to the increase in the relative price of imported
oil -- surely one of the "root causes" of current
economic problems of Portugal and most other oil im-
porting countries. It is difficult for non-economists to accept that the sharp increase of the price
of oil is in itself part of the solution to the
problem; probably one of the most effective remedies
over a period of time. The higher price of imported
oil will stimulate domestic production of alternative sources of energy, and it will also encourage
energy conservation. The possibilities for substitution are likely to be quite small in the short run
but even marginal adjustments by energy users and
producers contribute more to the solution of the
problem than empty rhetoric and elaborate plans and
programs. Over a period of time, high energy prices
force firms, and all other energy users, to reduce
the energy intensity of their activities by building
more energy-efficient production processes, machines,
transportation vehicles, factories and residential

buildings. The producers of the required capital
goods will have an incentive to design better and
more energy-efficient products for the ultimate
users. In the production of energy, also, long-
run supply potential is much greater than short-run
potential: high prices stimulate investment in
exploration, R&D in new technologies, and in required
expansion of domestic energy producing capacity.
"Energy problem," like most other economic problems,
can be solved only if everybody in society contrib-
utes to the solution: the market system gives the
incentive to everybody to try his or her best.

It is unlikely that the increase in the price
of oil and other energy resources is enough to
restore balance of payments equilibrium in a small
open economy that has only limited possibilities
for domestic energy production, even over a period
of time. But the solution of the balance of payments problem does not require additional measures
of energy policy either; rather, it requires appropriate exchange rate policy, and an appropriate
policy regarding foreign borrowing and capital
imports.

Suppose for simplicity that foreign borrowing
is not possible. Then, following an increase in
the price of oil, trade balance must be restored to
equilibrium by reducing the volume of oil imports,
by reducing other imports, and by increasing exports.
This can be done either by reducing the level of
domestic demand, by devaluing the currency, or by
a combination of the two. If wages are not indexed,
either explicitly or implicitly, devaluation is the
appropriate policy: it will further increase
domestic price of energy and thus encourage domestic
energy production and reduce energy consumption.
But devaluation will also reduce other imports and
increase exports, thus contributing to restoration
of balance of payments equilibrium through adjustments in all sectors, and by all individuals, firms
and farms in the economy. Devaluation will also
give additional incentives to investment in future
energy production and energy saving, as well as in
future production of exports and import-competing
goods.

This is how it should be. The necessity to pay
for more expensive oil imports requires a short-
term sacrifice, which society as a group cannot
escape from. The sacrifice takes many forms: a
reduction in oil imports, a reduction in energy consumption, a diversion of resources from other uses
to domestic production of energy; reduction of

imports other than oil; diversion of resources from other uses to the production of more exports; and also, diversion of resources from current consumption to investment, and thus to future consumption. Optimal response requires equality of marginal sacrifice: this is obtained by a policy that lets domestic energy prices reflect the true social cost of energy, and further lets the price of foreign exchange reflect the true social cost of foreign exchange: the marginal social cost of an additional dollar of imports, and the marginal social benefit of an additional dollar of exports.

In contrast, an energy policy response consisting, for example, of different kinds of subsidies to domestic energy production, puts the entire burden of adjustment on one sector of the economy, often in an arbitrary way, and is quite likely to lead to economic waste, and possibly also to an increase in required net imports of energy once all the general equilibrium effects are taken into account.

There is, of course, a role for government in the solution of the energy problem and thus a need for energy policy. But the case for specific policies must be based on a careful analysis of their costs and benefits, and of reasons why private markets cannot deal with the problem without government assistance or participation. It is not enough to say: the "energy crisis" is the "root cause" of economic problems, therefore the government must do everything it can to increase the population or to reduce the consumption of energy. This sort of response has political appeal but it is not the response of a rational society.

One reason for government intervention in solving the energy problem is that dependence on imported oil, with uncertain price and availability, imposes social and macroeconomic costs which private parties do not adequately take into consideration. Import dependence may also limit national independence by giving oil exporting countries the possibility of threatening with reduction or cutoff of supplies. The appropriate government policy to deal with the problem of import dependence is a quota, or tariff, on imports.

Another reason for government intervention in the solution of the energy problem are various externalities. Private investment in research and in development of new technologies is likely to be less than is socially optimal: subsidization of R&D is the appropriate policy. Many forms of energy have

148

serious environmental impacts, or are associated
with social risks: dealing with these problems
requires government policies.   Another reason for
government energy policy, particularly in small
countries, may be inability of the private sector
to raise the large amount of capital required in
many energy investments.

Similar considerations to these apply also to
other sectoral problems -- such as the problem of
agriculture emphasized by Stallings in her paper.
In every case it is important to analyze the nature
of the problem carefully, and in particular to
demonstrate why government intervention is needed.
Even the best of governments cannot solve all problems: it would be a good achievement if government managed "conventional macroeconomic policy"
well, and took care of only those problems that are
beyond the scope of competence of the private sector.

THE BURDEN OF STABILIZATION POLICIES

Stallings argues that orthodox stabilization
policies put the burden of adjustment on the working class: deflation puts workers out of work and
devaluation reduces their real earnings.   Other
measures, too, such as reduction of government
expenditure, and subsidies, also fall heavily on
the working class.

She is right: stabilization policies in
situations that she is discussing typically shift
income from wages to profits and lead to a period of
higher unemployment.   But if these policies succeed,
"working class" will benefit too from growth in
income, employment and real earnings.   Real wages
and distribution of income between labor and capital
are not variables that can be arbitrarily fixed by
government, as is often presumed by non-economists.
Thus, consider an extreme case of a small country
producing only internationally traded goods whose
prices are exogenously given in the world market.
Given the stock of capital in its various forms,
profit-maximizing firms will expand employment in
various industries up to the point of equality
between marginal revenue product and the nominal
wage rate.   Assuming, for simplicity, homogenous
labor force there is thus a unique wage rate consistent with full employment equilibrium in the
labor market.

If that is so, why not tax the capitalists and
use the proceeds either to subsidize employment, or
to finance lump sum transfers to workers?   This

would be possible if capital stayed in place, equally productive forever without investment and the
entrepreneurial contribution of capitalists. But
that is not the case: capital goods are not gifts
of nature but they are produced, and only if the
rate of return that they realize once in place
justifies cost of production with allowance for risk
and interest.

Thus, an increase in the wage rate above equilibrium not only increases unemployment in the short-
run but also reduces the rate of investment, and
thus reduces the equilibrium wage rate itself by
causing a continuous reduction in the ratio(s) of
productive capital to a growing labor force.

Open economies in which real wage demands exceed the "warranted real wage" will experience growing unemployment and slow growth: if unemployment
does not succeed in lowering real wages, there may
indeed be no other alternative but to assign "a
strong economic role to the state" not "to protect
workers' incomes" but to restore capital accumulation and growth.

INFLATION AND THE BALANCE OF PAYMENTS PROBLEM

Stallings argues in several places that inflation and balance of payments deficits are structural
problems which can be suppressed but not solved by
conventional macroeconomic policies. She does not,
however, provide an alternative beyond suggesting
the need for import controls and state intervention.

There is no question that inflation and balance
of payments deficits can be brought under control by
means of domestic credit policy irrespective of
national peculiarities; the only question is the
cost of deflationary policies in terms of unemployment and lost output during transition to lower
inflation and balance of payments equilibrium. The
cost may be so high that stabilization is politically impossible, or, if attempted, will lead to
social unrest or revolution. Unfortunately, economists cannot offer very good advice once economic
crisis has reached this point.

In many developing countries, stabilization
requires reduction or elimination of government
budget deficits, and thus either an increase in
taxes or a reduction in expenditures or transfer
payments -- all of which are likely to be met with
strong protest by affected groups. Devaluation,
and elimination or reduction of price subsidies are
also typically part of a stabilization package --

and equally unpopular. But there is no alternative -- unless something can be done to increase real resources available to a country.

It is true that there are many structural problems in developing and semi-industrialized countries, as Stallings argues in the case of Portugal, but the origin of many of these problems -- not all, however -- is government fiscal, monetary and exchange rate policy. To take the case of agriculture, which Stallings rightly emphasizes: a major reason for slow growth of agricultural output in many developing countries has been trade and exchange rate policy which has discriminated against agriculture in an attempt to stimulate import-competing manufacturing sectors. In other sectors, too, undervaluation of exchange rates, and attempts to suppress inflation by means of price controls, and to reduce balance of payments deficits by means of trade and foreign exchange controls, have gradually led to structural problems which later appear to be in need of structural remedies. Taken in isolation, such sector-specific policies seem often justified, and maybe even absolutely necessary, but taken in the proper context, such policies only add to the complexity of structural problems in the future.

IMPORT CONTROLS AND INWARD LOOKING DEVELOPMENT

Stallings calls for "unorthodox policies", by which she means import controls, and is critical of export-oriented policies. She refers to the new Cambridge macroeconomics as an intellectual justification of the closed economy model.

Whatever relevance "new Cambridge macroeconomics" may have in the solution of the United Kingdom's economic problems, and it is doubtful if it has any, it hardly has any relevance for a small country such as Portugal. The only two economic justifications for import controls and/or import tariffs are the optimal tariff argument on the one hand, and the national defense case for limiting import dependence on the other. The optimal tariff argument presupposes monopoly power in export markets and monopsony power in import markets, none of which presumably apply to Portugal, or for that matter to the United Kingdom either.

There is also a variant of the optimal tariff argument which appears under the surface of the new Cambridge macroeconomics. Suppose that a country, England for example, simply cannot compete in world markets: it can sell only to a certain number of

traditional customers, the others are not interested.
If the price is above the price of competitors, even
the traditional customer will not buy English
products; if it is below the competitors' price,
only the fixed number of traditional customers will
buy English products. Thus the demand schedule is
kinked, as is shown in Figure 3.1. If exports are
below their maximum potential level, devaluation
will lead to an increase in export volume with no
change in foreign currency prices: in Figure 3.1
the supply schedule shifts from SS to S'S' and the
volume of exports from E_1 to E_M. But after the maximum export potential has been reached at E_M, devaluation will not increase the volume of exports
at all: it will lead to a proportional decline in
export prices to P_2, and thus it will benefit
foreigners in an amount measured by the shaded area
(this analysis assumes that devaluation is not offset by domestic inflation).

In this situation export fed growth is self-
defeating, and thus one might argue growth of import-
competing industries is the only possibility. Import controls would shift demand towards domestic
output without increasing export supply and thus
without leading to a terms of trade deterioration.
Assuming that domestic demand for domestic products
is not linked in the same way as export demand, it
is possible to develop a formal model in which all
of this is true.

But upon closer scrutiny the case is extremely
weak. How can it ever be that growth potential is
greater in a small insulated market than it is in
the world market? Consider an individual in an
economy: his only possibility for material advance-
ment (and one might argue, for intellectual growth)
is to participate in trade; indeed, without trade,
an individual cannot survive.

In exactly the same way, a small country ex-
hausts its growth potential unless it participates
in trade. Welfare depends on availability and
consumption of a large number and broad variety of
products which are complementary in use. A small
economy cannot possibly produce all products and all
varieties of a given product: if the level of imports (and of course exports) does not grow, domestic material welfare will also stagnate.

Like in the case of an individual, the fundamental choice of a small country is whether to succeed or fail in (international) trade in goods,
services and ideas. There does not exist "an alternative development model."

152

FIGURE 3-1

Price of Exports and Export Volume

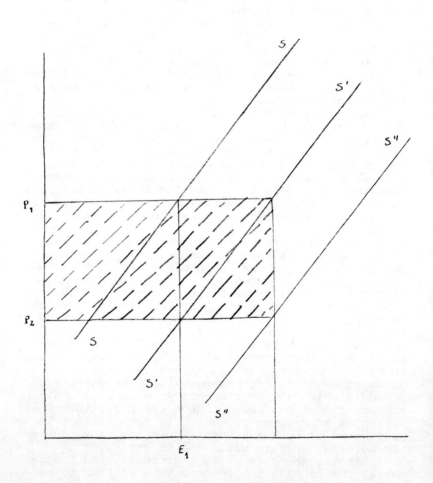

4
Portugal and Europe: The Channels of Structural Interdependence

Jorge Braga de Macedo

"Não é possivel considerar a vida portuguesa, ao longo de oito seculos em que enfrentou, com sucesso, tão diferentes situações, esquecendo a capacidade portuguesa de combinar, como Estado soberano, as vantagens politicas da sua independencia com as conveniencias europeias da colaboração."** Jorge Borges de Macedo, Uma perspectiva Portuguesa para a integração europeia, Instituto Democracia e Liberdade, Lisbon, 1977, page 9.

"Economic growth can be sustained by emigration and higher wages as well as by unlimited supplies of labor and constant wages", Charles Kindleberger, Europe's Postwar Growth, the role of the labor supply, Harvard University Press, Cambridge, 1967, p. 87.

---

*Comments from and conversations with Henry Bienen, Carlos Diaz, Albert Fishlow, Louka Katseli, Pentti Kouri, Paul Krugman and Antonio Labiza are gratefully acknowledged, naturally without implication.

**It is not possible to understand Portuguese life, for the eight centuries during which it confronted successfully such different situations, without understanding the Portuguese ability to combine, as a sovereign state, the political advantages of independence with the conveniences of European cooperation.

Portugal is becoming a member of the European
Economic Communities in a turbulent economic and
political environment which contrasts sharply with
the one prevailing from the treaties of Rome and
Stockholm to the first enlargement of the EEC.
Soon after the United Kingdom, Denmark and
Ireland joined the Six, the international economic
environment was shocked by the 1973 oil crisis and
the great recession of 1974-75. The hesitant
recovery was further undermined by the oil price
increases and supply disruptions of 1979. The
environment also suffered from a marked deterioration in the relations between the American and
Soviet superpowers. The Western nations are thus
confronted with continuing unemployment and inflation at home, a pressing need to conserve energy
and a greater concern for military security.
The end of three decades of full employment
growth has in turn complicated and slowed down the
process of European integration. The increasingly
divergent macroeconomic performance of West Germany
on the one hand and France, Italy, and the United
Kingdom, on the other, has been creating strains
among the members of the EEC. There are major
cleavages not only with respect to the new problems
of energy and military policy, but also relative to
the old objectives of coordinating monetary and
exchange rate policies in the European Monetary
System, reformulating the Common Agricultural
Policy and financing an expanded Community budget.
In Portugal, the domestic political and
economic environment was decisively affected by the
1974 Revolution. After a period of civil strife
where the ideological pressure was largely anti-
Western, the democratic government established in
the summer of 1976 requested membership in the EEC,
as promised during the electoral campaign. Economically, the shock of the oil embargo was followed,
after the Revolution, by severe wage inflation,
widespread nationalizations and expansionary fiscal
policies. The cumulative external imbalance that
came as a result of these policies led to a belated
but effective austerity program in 1978. So effective that it has prevented the recovery of private
investment and has widened the economic gap between
Portugal and Europe. The transitional inflow of
real resources necessary to avoid the adverse
effects of full economic integration will therefore
have to be larger than would be the case if the
"catching up" process had not been interrupted.

Portugal, however, is not joining the Community alone. Soon after the Portuguese Revolution, regimes inspired by the Western norm of political democracy were also established in Greece and neighboring Spain. Accordingly, membership in the EEC was requested in 1975 and 1977 respectively and the negotiations with Greece were concluded in May 1979.

Even if the integration of the new entrants would not require aid for the restoration of macroeconomic equilibrium and an acceleration of economic growth, the Southern enlargement would have a significant impact on the Community, particularly in problem areas such as agriculture and "sensitive" industries. But, as the provisions of the treaty of accession of Greece show, the necessity of such aid is acknowledged and further strains on the Community budget are to be expected.

Thus, contrary to the expectation of positive short and medium run effects of European economic integration that led the original Six to set up the Common Market and to enlarge it in the early seventies, the expectation is that the current enlargement is more likely to have negative short and medium run effects on the Community as well as on its prospective members. On the other hand, the deterioration of the international political environment, without reviving the federalist dreams of the early days, has generated a sense of fundamental European solidarity which made the second enlargement imperative.

Such a steep trade-off between political and economic incentives was absent in the earlier experience of the European Community which was largely based on the hope for consolidation of economic gains from increased structural interdependence into policy interdependence and ultimately political integration.

While the trade-off exists for the present members of the Community as well as for the new applicants, it is perhaps most dramatic in the case of Portugal. Since the Revolution, in effect, Portugal has become at the same time politically closer to the European Community and economically more distant from it. It is argued in this paper that Portugal benefitted from Europe's postwar growth by directing manufacturing exports and providing labor to a more advanced area. These benefits can be ascertained by a continuous increase in the real wage and an unusually strong balance of payments position.

The sensitivity to (marginal) economic developments abroad was thus greater at the time the 1972 free trade agreement with the EEC was signed than it is now or is likely to become in the near future. However, the domestic and international macroeconomic malaise did not prevent the EEC from showing a political responsiveness to Portuguese integration that was lacking then. To the point that "Europe is with us" became a major political slogan in the 1976 elections and that the government appointed after the December 1979 elections called European integration "the priority of priorities".

As the first opening quote suggests, the approach followed in this paper takes as given a national cultural identity that cannot be "integrated". Even if increased structural and policy interdependence and mutual political responsiveness does feed back on some European, or Western, sociocultural homogeneity, "in which the separate cultures are held to coexist"[1], the privileged domain of political and cultural identification remains the nationstate. In other words, if the only way for European integration to enlarge the consumption possibilities of the Portuguese population would be for it to massively leave the country, and the exodus would indeed take place, Portuguese cultural identity, as defined here, would be more likely to disappear than to coexist with the cultures of the host countries. The preservation of the Portuguese cultural identity will therefore be taken to enter the collective welfare of the Portuguese population.

The paper is organized into seven sections. Section 1 makes some comparisons between the EEC and the three candidates, together with comparisons of the candidates with each other.

While the latter comparisons show a fairly similar pattern of increased structural interdependence between the Nine and the three candidates via international trade and investment and labor migration, the failure to transform traditional agriculture is a singularly perverse feature of Portugal and is taken up in Section 2.

The next three sections analyze the main channels of economic interdependence between Portugal and the EEC. Section 3 describes the structure of foreign trade, emphasizing the growth of exports of manufactures in the sixties. Section 4 is devoted to foreign direct investment and its link with the export boom. Section 5 discusses emigration and the effects of migrants remittances on growth and the balance of payments.

The effects of interdependence, particularly emigration, on the process of growth with increasing real wages are taken up in Section 6. The implications of trends in the distribution of income in the early seventies for the macroeconomic difficulties that followed the Revolution are also analyzed.

Section 7 looks at the effects of structural interdependence on the prospects for "political integration". In line with the notion of cultural identity adopted in the paper, attempts at using structural variables to determine the "rational choice" of countries seeking to integrate are criticized at first. An overview of Portuguese foreign economic policy in the post war period and of the political and bureaucratic process that has led to seeking membership follows and it is used to interpret some evidence on societal attitudes about European integration. While outside the scope of the paper, brief mention is made of the wide range of issues, from fiscal harmonization to monetary integration, that pertain to the degree of policy interdependence between Portugal and the EEC.

The conclusion stresses again that the economic development of the territory is a crucial condition for the nation's cultural identity to survive European integration.

1. THE NINE, SOUTHERN EUROPE AND PORTUGAL

The economic homogeneity of the European Community at the time of the treaty of Rome in 1958 was certainly a major factor in the success of the establishment of a Customs Union in 1968, one and a half years ahead of the original schedule.[2] Countries with similar resource endowments, in effect, tend to engage in intra-industry trade, so that the distributional implications familiar from conventional trade theory are absent.[3]

The first enlargement created some preoccupation, not only because of the relative underdevelopment of Ireland and the special ties of the United Kingdom with the Commonwealth but also because of the inflationary pressures that had emerged in the late sixties. It turned out that Ireland was able to attract substantial direct investment but the other two concerns were indeed warranted. The

"integration" of the U.K. in the Community has
been painful for both and, of course, inflation,
from being a reversible consequence of U.S. monetary
policy, is now coupled with unemployment and a
serious energy problem.

The reduced economic capabilities of the EEC
have been associated with a greater contrast between
"strong" economies, such as Germany, and "weak"
economies such as Italy, the U.K. and possibly
France. Both tend to bring to the fore difficult
distributional issues within countries and at the
Community level that were absent in the earlier
period.

Furthermore, it is in the areas where stages
beyond the Customs Union were attempted, such as
agriculture and the coordination of monetary and
exchange rate policies, that the most severe
strains have developed.

The political commitment to a United Europe,
which was crucial to launch the economic enterprise
in the fifties, has nevertheless become such that
the European Community is in the process of inte-
grating its southern periphery.[4]

In fact, a well known document of the Commission[5] emphasized that Southern Europe appears as a
relatively homogeneous semi-industrialized region
in the following dimensions: (1) a level of
development considerably lower than the community
average; (2) large scale and growing regional disequilibria; (3) considerable weight of agriculture
in production and employment; (4) broadly similar
structure in industrial production and particularly
industrial exports; (5) very marked orientation of
external trade toward the Community; (6) substantial
source of labor for the Community; (7) high level
of investment since the mid-sixties; (8) considerable structural underemployment; (9) importance of
foodstuffs in the structure of private consumption;
and (10) lack of infrastructure and a relatively
low share of public expenditure in gross national
product.

These common features "increase the problems
which the new Community of Twelve will face in
restoring growth and improving cohesion".[6]

In particular, the complex and expensive system of price subsidies of the Common Agricultural
Policy makes the accession of largely agricultural
countries particularly burdensome for the Community
and the member countries. The second enlargement,
in fact, will imply a 56 percent increase in agricultural employment but only a 24 percent increase

in agricultural production (in dollars). In 1975,
agricultural output per man was $6.8 million dol-
lars in the EEC and 3.2 in the three applicants
(2.1 in Portugal), so that the Community of Twelve
average would be $5.5[7]. The expected increase in
southern agricultural productivity will then imply
substantial reallocation of labor to other sectors.
This availability of labor for industry and
services could generate a Lewis-type growth process
in the enlarged Community, like it did in the EEC
and its southern periphery in the fifties and sixties[8]. The current prospect, however, is that it
will imply a worsening of the existing unemployment
problem. In fact, if migration and capital mobility
reinforce the tendency for factor price equaliza-
tion through trade in goods and services, or if
increasing returns to scale are widespread, manufacturing may disappear from the peripheral countries, worsening the disparity between the community
and the new entrants.

The unequalizing process of expanded international trade and investment, which is familiar
from the Marxian perspective on the development of
a "world capitalist economy", is not only a
theoretical consequence of the Second Enlargement.[9]
The overall homogeneity of the Six original members
of the EEC notwithstanding, regional disparities
there have certainly not declined. Even in pros-
perous Germany the range of per capita incomes
across regions increased by 1.5 between 1957 and
1970[10]. This uneven development has occurred despite policies designed to prevent it, which are
basically the responsibility of member countries.
Given the serious regional disparities in the new
applicant countries and the limited resources that
they would be able to commit to that objective, it
is not difficult to assert that the "golden triangle" of the enlarged EEC will continue to have
vertices in Birmingham, Dusseldorf, and Milan[11].

From the viewpoint of macroeconomic stabilization, if the member countries also forego exchange
policy they will only be able to rely on fiscal
contraction and deflation to correct a payments
deficit[12]. In fact, in the case where the factor
price frontier and the price of the traded goods are
given, the peripheral economy's fate is completely
determined from outside. Slow growth in the center
will, therefore, increase the difficulty in dupli-
cating successfully policies of "exploitative
interdependence" such as the ones that Ireland was
able to implement[13].

This discussion can be illustrated with some rough comparative indicators about the performance of the present European Community and the three Southern European candidates from the early sixties to the mid-seventies, presented in Table 4.1. While the figures on productivity growth and the investment share in the European periphery are probably not accurate, it is clear from the Table that output (line 1) and output per employed worker (line 2) have grown there at a rate higher than the EEC average. The investment share in GDP (line 3) is, however, lowest in Portugal. Thus, in 1960-75, it is the country with the lowest output per capita that has the lowest rate of output growth of the three candidates. The same occurs with respect to productivity in the sixties. In the early seventies, however, productivity growth is reported to be over 5 percent p.a., in Portugal and Greece, which is twice as high as the figures of the EEC and Spain[14].

The growth rates of the late seventies are accordingly higher in Portugal and Greece. However, in 1977 GDP per capita in Portugal was still at the 1973 level, because the 9 percent increase in the population due to the inflow of returnees from the African territories in 1974-75 offset the growth of output.

In the sectoral distribution of employment in the early seventies (line 4), Greece stands out with a much higher share of agriculture (and fisheries) than the two other applicants, which have a share comparable to the one of Ireland (25 percent). Similarly, the shares of manufacturing and services to Spain, and even in Portugal, are closer to the Nine than to Greece. This rough pattern is misleading, however, because it is in Portugal that, as we pointed out, the decline of agriculture is more alarming[15].

2. THE PROBLEM OF AGRICULTURE

Despite a long tradition of exporting skilled labor intensive wine products from the Douro valley, Portuguese agriculture remained largely traditional during the post war period. As trade in manufactures, labor emigration and foreign direct investment were generating a process of export led growth, the contribution of agriculture declined from about one-fourth in the 1940's to 4 percent in the sixties (Table 4.2, Column 1). In 1960,

TABLE 4.1
The Nine and Southern Europe: Comparative
Indicators

	Portugal	Greece	Spain	EEC(9)
1. Growth of Gross Domestic Product (% p.a.)				
1969-70	6.3	7.6	7.5	4.7
1970-75	4.7	5.1	5.4	2.5
1975-80*	4.2**	4.1	2.0	3.0
2. Growth of Productivity (% p.a.)				
1960-70	5.5	8.3	6.7	4.4
1970-75	5.4	4.9	2.7	2.6
3. Gross Fixed Capital Formation/ GDP (%)				
1961-70	17.4	22.4	20.5	22.2
1971-75	18.6	23.8	23.3	22.2
4. Sectoral shares of employment in 1971-75 (%)				
Agriculture	27.8	38.9	24.8	10.3
Manufacturing	33.7	26.3	37.2	40.3
Services	38.5	34.8	38.1	49.4

Sources: European Commission Bulletin, Supplement
3/78.

 * Data and forecasts from OECD, Economic Outlook,
   December 1979.
** 1976-79 data from Banco de Portugal.

furthermore, the agricultural trade surplus turned into a deficit and its share in the total deficit increased steadily, to an average of 10 percent over the decade (Table 4.2, Column 2).

The productivity of labor in Portuguese agriculture, already noted as being the lowest by far of the three applicants, is also very low relative to the productivity of labor in other sectors. Thus the Kuznets "intersectoral ratio", which was close to two in 1950, increased to almost three in 1975, a level typical of countries with a very low GDP per capita. The typical tendency as GDP per capita goes up is, of course, for that ratio to become closer to one[16].

Agricultural employment declined by 35 percent over the period 1960-75. Had it remained constant, however, real value added would have increased at an annual rate of one half of one percent. The lack of investment in agriculture is responsible for this stagnation. When emigration was largest, the share of gross fixed capital formation in agricultural GDP was below 10 percent[17].

There were, nevertheless, instances of transformation of traditional agriculture, in particular the success stories of tomato concentrate and paper pulp, exports of which to the EEC were multiplied by a factor of forty and twenty-four respectively over the decade, while to EFTA the factors were nine and four respectively. Some modernization also occurred in the production of meat and fruit for the domestic market[18].

In any event, as shown in Table 4.2, the situation deteriorated further in the seventies. Agriculture had, on an average, a negative contribution to growth of about 5 percent and the agricultural share of the trade deficit rose to 18 percent. Figures for the years after the Revolution would be even worse. In 1975, agricultural output declined by 7 percent and the agricultural share of the trade deficit shot up to 30 percent. In 1977, output declined by 10 percent but due to the high trade deficit, the agriculture share dropped to 20 percent[19]. Bad harvests certainly played a part in the decline of crops in 1976 and 1977, but the chaotic "Agrarian Reform" conducted by the Communist Party in the Southern Provinces of Alentejo in the Summer of 1975 had a decisive negative impact on output and productivity. At the same time, wage increases in the urban sector swelled the demand for food so that agricultural imports rose by 25 percent in 1976 and 50 percent in 1977.

TABLE 4.2
The Decline of Portuguese Agriculture

	(1) Contribution of Agriculture to Growth (%)	(2) Share of Agriculture in the Trade Deficit (%)
1940-50	22.6	n.a.
1950-60	7.8	-8.4*
1960-70	3.9	9.8
1970-78	-4.8	18.0

Sources:
(1) Data to 1976 from A. Lobão, Agricultura portu-
    guese e integração europeia, Economia, May
    1979. 1977-78 Banco de Portugal.
(2) * 1956-59. Data to 1974 from World Bank, Portu-
    gal. Agricultural Sector Survey, November 1978.
    1975-78 Banco de Portugal.

Note: Agriculture includes crops, wine, fruits
and vegetables and forestry.

The political effects of the Agrarian Reform
were also decisive[20]. To begin with, they prevented
an attack on the problem of small low-output farms
in the North. According to the 1968 Census of
Agriculture, three-fourths of the land holdings
were under 4 ha of area and 39 percent under 1 ha,
whereas .5 percent of the farms--about 4700--held
45 percent of the land in units of 100 ha or larger.
About 500 "collective units of production" (UCP)
are still controlling 25 percent of the land in
units of 100 ha or larger. In the three main dis-
tricts of the Agrarian Reform--Beja, Evora and
Portalegre[21]--the UCP area per work is 30.7, over
twice what it was in 1970.

Attempts by successive non-Communist governments to break up these units faced strong resistance and led to major parliamentary crises in
the summers of 1978 and 1979. The greater deter-
mination of the government appointed after the
December 1979 elections notwithstanding, agriculture
is likely to remain a serious economic and social
problem in Portugal.

Aside from the already mentioned lower agricultural productivity in Portugal (74 percent
relative to Spain and Greece in the mid-seventies
and 34 percent relative to the Nine), farmed area
per worker was 56 percent relative to Greece and
about 40 percent relative to Spain and the Nine.
The same holds for area productivity. In wheat it
was about the same as in Greece, over half of the
Spanish figure and 23 percent of the French. In
rice, on the other hand, productivity was about the
same as in Spain and higher than in France but it
was 79 percent of the Greek figure. In wine, area
productivity in Portugal is about the same as in
Greece, but 58 percent of the Spanish figure, half
of the Italian and less than half the French. In
terms of fertilizers, Portugal is 80 percent below
Greece and 44 percent below Spain in nitrogen use.
The irrigated share of the cultivated area is
higher than in Greece but almost half of the
Spanish figure[22].

Agricultural trade between the three applicants
and the EEC is quite asymmetric. Ninety percent
of Portugal's agricultural exports are directed to
the EEC (50 percent for Spain and 60 percent for
Greece), whereas the EEC share in agricultural
imports is only 19 percent (28 percent for Spain
and 17 percent for Greece). The reason for the
lower import share is, of course, that the Common
Agricultural Policy has resulted in trade diversion

in all temperate zone ("northern") products,
particularly cereals[23]. On the export share, however, the applicants' agricultural products have
had access to the European market thanks to various
trading arrangements. As a consequence of these
preferences, there are less static gains from full
membership for producers to be expected than would
have been the case if agricultural exports would
have been subject to EEC external tariffs,[24] but
they can nevertheless be substantial if the CAP
price does not fall. Conversely, consumers in the
three applicant countries will clearly lose from
the higher prices of agricultural imports.
    For Portugal, there is evidence that producers
of corn, rice, and olive oil will benefit from CAP
prices, whereas less efficient producers of wheat
and milk will suffer and all "grain-beef" production will be competed away by more efficient EEC
farms. The comparative advantage of Portugal in
agricultural products involves a similar ranking.
In fact, at world prices, grain-fed livestock
production has negative value added[25]. On the
other hand, the Community reference will imply
higher prices for Portuguese consumers and therefore a substantial increase in the current subsidies until real incomes grow sufficiently to
absorb the higher price of food in the EEC.
    These prospects are, however, dependent on a
substantial effort in spreading the modernization
of Portuguese agriculture. The inability to do so
has had severe costs both on the short run macroeconomic adjustment process, via the balance of
payments, inflation and unemployment, and on the
probable effects of European integration. This
makes the political constraints that have prevented
agricultural recovery costly indeed.

3. FOREIGN TRADE AND INDUSTRIAL GROWTH

    The structure of Portugal's balance of payments
has been characterized over the centuries by a
merchandise trade deficit covered by unrequited
transfers and the monetization of bullion. In the
sixties, emigrants' remittances, receipts from
tourism and, later, foreign direct investment
increased to such a degree that substantial gold
reserves were accumulated. During that period, the
rapid expansion of exports was matched by increased
imports. Thus, in the late fifties the proportions
of merchandise exports and imports to gross domestic

product were 13 percent and 18 percent, whereas the
figures for the early seventies were 16 percent and
27 percent respectively[26].

The leading sector during this period was
manufacturing, the share of which in gross domestic
product climbed from 30 percent to 35 percent
between 1963 and 1973, while output was growing an
average of 7 percent p.a. Sources of direct growth
in manufacturing during the period were domestic
demand expansion (71 percent) and export expansion
(45 percent), while import substitution made a
negative contribution of 16 percent of manufacturing output growth[27]. Export growth, in turn, was
clearly associated with the participation in the
European Free Trade Agreement. While exports grew
at 9 percent p.a. in volume (and 11 percent in dollar terms as shown in the last row of Table 4.3)
during the sixties, exports to EFTA grew at 16 percent p.a. in volume.

The evolution of Portugal's main exports from
1963 to 1975 is reported in Table 4.3 by SITC
categories. Food exports, including wine (SITC 03
+ 05 + 1121) declined from 22.2 percent in 1963 to
12.3 percent in 1975. The same occurred with wood,
cork, and its manufactures (24 + 63) which declined
from 17.4 percent to 8.3 percent in the same period
while paper exports (64) increased. The most significant export is still textiles (65) which
nevertheless declined from 22.2 percent to 16.1
percent while clothing and footwear (84 + 851) increased from 4.3 percent to 13 percent. The remaining items include chemicals (5) metallic (69)
and non-metallic (66) manufactures, machinery (71),
particularly electric (72) and transport equipment
(73). Together they increased from 17 percent to
47 percent during the period.

It is therefore clear that a process of re-
placement of traditional exports of "light"
manufactures like textiles by "heavier" manufactures
has been going on. Available evidence on the physical and human capital intensities of Portuguese
exports confirms that they increased substantially
during the period, in particular the latter. Nevertheless, almost one-third of Portuguese exports in
1975 were still accounted for by textiles, clothing
and footwear.

While the EFTA agreement allowed Portugal to
postpone dismantling her own trade banners, the
fact that tariffs on most products were specific
led to a substantial erosion of protection when
world prices began to increase in the mid-sixties;

TABLE 4.3
Main Exports (%)

SITC	1963	1973	1975
03	10.5	3.4	2.7
05	4.3	5.6	2.9
1121	7.4	6.9	6.7
24	6.9	4.2	3.5
63	10.5	5.2	4.8
64	0.7	0.8	2.3
65	22.2	17.7	16.1
84	3.6	10.6	11.3
851	0.7	1.2	1.6
69	2.2	2.4	2.5
71	1.7	4.2	4.0
72	1.2	6.6	7.2
73	0.5	2.4	2.0
67	1.0	0.9	1.8
66	2.6	8.0	5.8
5	7.7	5.8	6.5
Total	83.7	85.9	81.9
Value of total exports (=100%) in million 1973 dollars	565	1862	1426

Source: UN Yearbook of International Trade Statistics, 1975.

Notes:
A description of SITC categories is found in the
Appendix Table.
Dollar exports deflated by U.S. Wholesale Price
Index 1973=1.

so that by the early seventies the average nominal
tariff was less than 10 percent. Based on the
1974 input-output matrix, Table 4.4 reports rates
of nominal and effective protection for three broad
categories of traded goods. While the nominal rate
is probably overstated, since it does not include
the effect of exemptions (which are believed to
be widespread), it is interesting to note that when
domestic import competing inputs are valued at
world prices (effective rate two), consumption and
investment goods industries had about the same rate
of protection in 1974, but the latter were substantially more protected after the 1976 surcharge.

Furthermore, taking into account that investment goods are mostly imported--the ratio of imports to total trade in that category being around
.8--we can see that investment goods were also more
penalized than consumption goods. In fact, the
premium implicit in the effective rate of protection and the trade structure is substantially
higher for investment goods (56 percent using
effective rate one and 47 percent using effective
rate two) than for intermediate goods (respectively
30 percent and 28 percent) or for consumer goods
(respectively 28 percent and 20 percent).[28]

Taking into account that the import content of
domestic investment is about 45 percent, whereas
the import content of consumption is only 25 percent[29], the justification of the higher premiums
on investment goods on balance of payments grounds
only dramatizes the trade-off between short run
adjustment and long run growth objectives that
policy makers were facing at the time of the import
surcharge.

Table 4.5 describes the direction of Portugal's
trade in 1976 and the extraordinary importance of
Europe, in particular the EEC, is apparent on the
export as well as the import side with over 51 and
41 percent respectively. Even though the low share
of the former African territories is a direct
consequence of decolonization it had declined on
the export side from 30 percent in the late fifties
to 24 percent in the late sixties. Similarly, the
import share remained fairly constant at 15 percent.

The structure of trade in manufactures between
the Nine and the three southern European candidates
in 1976 can be condensed by means of a rough indicator of comparative advantage, obtained by comparing
the share of exports and imports of commodity in
total exports and imports respectively.[30] If the
index in Table 4.6 is positive, the country tends

TABLE 4.4
Structure of Protection (%)

	1974 Tariff			1974 Tariff + 1976 Surcharge		
	Nominal Rate	Effective 1	Rate 2	Nominal Rate	Effective 1	Rate 2
Consumption goods	13	24	15	31	59	43
Intermediate goods	8	14	10	26	40	37
Investment goods	10	17	14	40	67	58

Source: Adapted from Toscano, cit. p. 53 with data from 1974 input-output matrix of Grupo de Estudos Basicos de Economia Industrial (GEBEI).

Notes:
Nominal rate: tariff revenues/imports.
Effective rate 1: tradable but not traded inputs valued at domestic prices.
Effective rate 2: tradable but not traded inputs valued at world prices.

170

TABLE 4.5
Direction of Trade in 1976 (%)

Country	Imports	Exports
Europe	58.31	71.73
Community	41.47	51.47
FR Germany	11.60	10.74
France	8.61	8.37
Italy	4.67	3.75
Netherlands	3.74	3.40
Belgium-Lux	2.73	3.46
United Kingdom	9.31	18.40
Ireland	0.18	0.46
Denmark	0.63	2.89
Spain	4.20	2.10
Sweden	3.06	7.68
Switzerland	3.39	2.78
USSR	2.37	2.99
Africa	6.22	8.45
Angola	.94	1.59
Mozambique	1.12	1.49
America	14.94	10.44
United States	9.82	6.74
Brazil	1.05	1.01
Asia	17.12	4.01
Japan	3.20	1.15
Saudi Arabia	3.63	0.06
Iraq	3.85	0.24
Iran	2.65	0.25
Other	3.41	5.37

Source: Same as Table 4.3.

TABLE 4.6
Indices of "Revealed Comparative Advantage" in Manufactures in 1976: The Nine and Southern Europe

SITC	PORT	EEC	GR	SP	SITC	PORT	EEC	GR	SP
51	-228.4	-7.2	-25.4	-96.4	66	108.9	-12.2	209.6	54.3
52		-97.0		-76.8	67	-87.3	2.3	77.6	6.4
53	-200.5	34.1	-220.4	-107.4	68	-260.4	-71.2	136.8	-32.4
54	-110.9	21.5	-87.9	-114.8	(69)	11.8	20.1	86.6	95.2
55	-74.9	16.2	2.9	-3.3	71	-144.9	26.6	-259.6	-81.9
56	131.2	-18.2	-94.1	137.9	72	-11.9	4.3	-34.5	-61.6
57	78.8	17.5	-55.6	-4.9	73	-112.4	25.2	-241.3	89.9
58	-265.4	6.2	-70.3	-131.7	(81)	6.2	-4.0	26.2	49.4
59	85.4	14.0	65.8	-94.1	82	-89.1	-8.3	59.8	133.2
(61)	44.9	-39.0	119.4	98.5	(83)	67.5	-35.9	174.7	210.6
62	-91.9	11.1	-103.5	168.1	(84)	311.8	-62.2	418.1	148.8
(63)	450.2	-71.5	152.6	185.0	(85)	415.5	-17.8	580.7	398.8
64	107.6	-77.7	-164.4	-12.2	86	-93.0	-16.8	-243.3	-217.2
(65)	150.0	-18.1	172.4	47.3	89	-44.3	-11.2	38.8	61.0

Source: Adapted from Donges-Schatz op. cit.

Notes:
A description of the SITC categories is found in the Appendix Table.
Underlined SITC codes: comparative disadvantage for all three applicants.
SITC codes in parentheses: comparative advantage for all three applicants.

to export rather than to import that commodity
(relative to the total exports and imports) and is
therefore taken to reveal comparative advantage in
the production of the commodity in question. It
is clear that "real" comparative advantage cannot
be derived from actual trade figures because the
index reflects trade distortions like tariffs on
imports or subsidies on exports. Accordingly, as
far as Portugal is concerned, comparisons of the
index over time are bound to reflect the effects of
trade liberalization in the context of EFTA and of
the 1972 free trade agreement with the EEC.[31]
     With these caveats in mind, the similarities
of the three Southern countries are apparent in
the comparative advantage for leather, wood and
cork, textiles, small appliances, travel goods,
clothing and footwear, the SITC code of which is
circled, and the comparative disadvantage for dying
products (53), medical products (54), plastic
materials (58), rubber manufactures (62), electric
and non-electric machinery (71 and 72), and transport equipment (73), the SITC code of which is
underlined. The only range of products where all
countries reveal a comparative advantage are sundry
manufactures of metal (SITC 69). The only group
of products for which Portugal alone reveals a
comparative advantage are paper manufactures (64)
and the index is the highest of the four for
chemical materials (59) and wood and cork (63). On
the other hand Portugal is the only one to reveal
comparative disadvantage in iron and steel (67) and
has the lowest value for chemical elements (51),
perfumes (55), plastics (58), non-ferrous metals
(68) and miscellaneous manufactures (89).
     Portugal reveals therefore a pattern of simul-
taneous comparative advantage in primary products
and unskilled-labor-intensive manufactures on the
one hand and manufactures with a higher (physical
and human) capital intensity, on the other. This
is, of course, a typical pattern for a semi-
industrialized economy[32].

4. FOREIGN DIRECT INVESTMENT

     From 1962 to 1973, as we pointed out, migrants'
remittances more than offset the traditional
Portuguese trade deficit, so that the current
account was in surplus. Both in 1961 and since
1974, the current account deficits were financed
mostly by transactions of the monetary institutions.

However, since the early sixties Portugal often
recorded surpluses on the non-monetary capital
account, in particular via foreign direct investment. Aside from its relative importance in the
private capital account, contrasting with other
Southern European countries[33], direct investment
is an important channel of structural interdependence because of its role in the transfer of
technology.

Despite a very high rate of growth in the late
sixties and early seventies, the stock of foreign
direct investment in Portugal remained small in
comparison with other Southern European countries.
In 1970, for instance, U.S. direct investment per
capita was $15 in Portugal, $22 in Spain, $38 in
Italy, and $144 in Great Britain.[34] Total annual
flows, about $30 million in 1971, reached over $62
million in 1978, below the pre-revolutionary peak
of $85 million in 1973. Of these, $35 million
represented the formation of new companies, which
after declining to less than half in 1975 (the 1971
value) was back at that rate in 1977 and increased
slightly in 1978. The book value of foreign direct
investment for that year was estimated to be about
$400 million, or 5 percent of the total investments
of developed OECD countries in the Southern European Area (including Turkey and Yugoslavia).[35]

In the total stock, the EEC had a share of 50
percent, whereas the U.S. share was 20 percent.
The shares of flows, shown in Table 4.7, vary
widely often due to individual operations. The
divestment of the U.K., which once had the largest
share, started in the late 60's. Germany divested
significantly after 1975 and France never had a
significant share. The 1977 EEC share is therefore from the smaller member countries. "Other
OECD" includes not only Canada and Japan, which
have been negligible in the last few years, but
also the mini-EFTA, in particular Switzerland,
which increased her share from 9 percent in 1975
and 11 percent in 1976 to 27 percent in 1977. The
share of the U.S. which was at a low in 1973 also
increased in the following years, whereas the
importance of the Rest of the World declined.

For contrast, we might consider the shares
of the proposals submitted to the recently established Institute of Foreign Investment in 1979.[36]
Here the substantial difference in shares is
accounted for by different definitions and cover-
ages aside from the effect of individual proposals.
For example, Sweden jumped from a share of 2.2

TABLE 4.7
Foreign Direct Investment by Country of Origin %

	1969	1971	1973	1975	1977	1979
U.S.	23	25	8.8	27.3	25.4	8.7
U.K.	23	10	62.6	41.3	40.2	37.1
EEC (6)	26	27	19.8	11.5	31.3	40.0
Other OECD	25	27	8.8	19.8	3.0	15.2
Rest of World	4	11				

Sources:
1969-71 Macedo Interdependencia, cit., p. 293.
1973-77 Banco de Portugal Annual Reports.
1979   IIE, Investimento Estrangeiro em Portugal 1978/79.

Note: 1979 refers to proposals to the Institute of Foreign Investment (IIE) and is not comparable with earlier figures.

percent in 1978 to 14.3 percent in 1979 with only
three operations.

The major sector of destination of foreign
direct investment has been manufacturing (27 percent in 1972-76 and 42 percent in 1977-78), followed by trade and tourism (20 percent in 1972-74,
31 percent in 1975-76 and 37.6 percent in 1977-78).
Within manufacturing, sectors with annual rates of
export growth higher than 20 percent[37] such as
electronics, paper, rubber, chemicals and metal-
works accounted for 57 percent of foreign direct
investment by 200 firms in the early seventies.
This export bias is confirmed by the analysis of
the relative performance of domestic and foreign
firms in textiles and electrical components[38].

5.   EMIGRATION, REMITTANCES AND THE BALANCE OF
     PAYMENTS

     Portuguese emigration resumed soon after the
end of the second world war and reached 24 thousand
workers in 1952. It declined later in the decade
and did not attain the 1952 peak until 1963. In
1964, however, it went over 50 thousand and continued to increase until 1970, when 100 thousand
workers left the country. Total emigration,
including families, was about 1.5 times higher.
In the early seventies, while the outflow of
workers declined, the family factor increased to
two.[39]

     Table 4.8 provides comparative information on
the relative sizes of foreign workers in the main
EEC countries and the relative importance of emigration for the peripheral countries in the mid-
seventies. It is clear that the preferred host
country of Portuguese emigrants is France (81 percent) and that Portugal has by far the highest
share of foreign workers in domestic employment.

     Despite the importance of emigration, the
differential between the Portuguese wage and a
weighted average of the main host countries to
Portuguese remained substantial. Indeed, it may
have increased: it was estimated to be of the
order of 1/17 in 1953 and 1/20 in 1972[40]. Since
1973 the differential in real wages narrowed and
then widened, in a pattern similar to the one of
the domestic real wage (see Chart 4.3 below),
except that the increase was never higher than 7
percent in late 1974 and that, having returned to
the base value in late 1975, it was less than 80

TABLE 4.8
Southern European Workers in the EEC in 1975 (thousands)

Host Country / Country of Origin	Benelux	France	Germany	Nether-lands	United Kingdom	Total as % of Employment in Country of Origin
Portugal	15.5	430.0	70.0	5.0	4.0	17.3
Greece	8.0	5.0	212.0	2.0	2.5	7.2
Spain	31.9	250.0	132.0	18.0	15.5	3.5
Total as % of Employment in Host Country	10.2	9.9	8.5	4.7	3.1	
Memo: Total as % of foreign workers in host country	17.1	36.1	18.9	11.6	2.8	20.3

Source: Adapted from Z. Ecevit and K. Zachariah, "International Labor Migration", Finance and Development, December 1978, p. 33 using data from OECD, SOPEMI, Continuous Reporting System on Migration, 1976.

percent thereof three years later.[41]

Nevertheless, the effects on the steady-state rate of growth of the economy would have been quite unfavorable if remittances would not have increased domestic savings substantially.[42] But Portugal received consistently higher remittances per capita than other Mediterranean labor-exporting countries[43], and in 1972, remittances reached 26 percent of foreign exchange receipts and 38 percent of reserve money[44].

As mentioned above, a dramatic change occurred with the world recession, since emigration stopped and remittances in current dollars ceased to increase in 1974 to actually decline in 1975 when over half a million refugees--about the same number as the emigrants in Table 4.8--were returning from the former colonies. The political stabilization of 1976-77 notwithstanding, remittances only increased when interest rates were substantially raised in 1978[45].

Since aggregate expenditure is equal to national income--inclusive of remittances--less the current account, the evolution of the economy over time can be interpreted by comparing the deficit on goods and services to the surplus on unrequited transfers.[46] This is done in Chart 4.1 for the period 1959-1979, using the U.S. wholesale price index as a deflator to obtain values in units of purchasing power over U.S. goods. Until 1965, the current account was in deficit but, except for 1961, when the incidents in Angola led to an extraordinary increase in the deficit on goods and services, the gap between income and expenditure was not too large. As remittances start to increase continuously between 1965 and 1973, income becomes larger than expenditure. The combined effect of the increase in the real trade deficit and the decline in real remittances in 1974 was to create a huge income-expenditure gap, which was only corrected in 1979, due to the substantial increase in real remittances.

The evolution of the Portuguese balance on non-monetary transactions is documented in Chart 4.2, using the same deflator as previously.[47] Private capital movements, unlike remittances, have not been as important in Portugal as in other Mediterranean countries, but the banking sector and the Treasury accumulated foreign exchange consistently from 1962 to 1973. Reserves were also increased by some precautionary foreign borrowing by the State while post-war legislation enhanced

CHART 4-1
COMPONENTS OF THE CURRENT ACCOUNT
(millions of 1973 dollars)

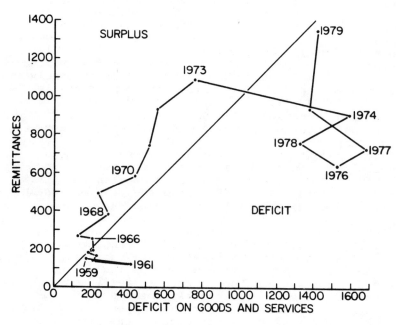

Sources: 1959-63   Goods and Services from IFS National
Accounts; Remittances from Barbosa, op.cit.,
series (3) both converted into dollars at the
rate $1 = 28.75
1964-1979:   Banco de Portugal Annual Reports (1978
and 1979 preliminary)
Deflated by U.S. wholesale price index from IFS,
1973 = 1

CHART 4-2
BALANCE ON NON-MONETARY TRANSACTIONS
(millions of 1973 dollars)

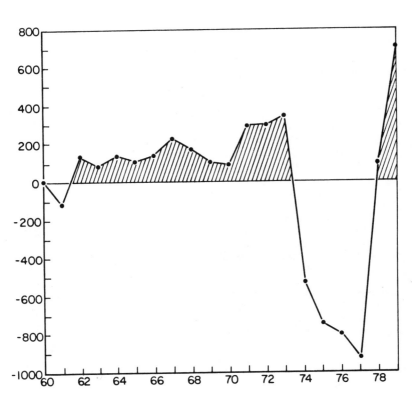

Sources: 1960-1974 OECD, Balance of Payments of OECD
countries 1960-77, Paris, January 1979, using
data from Banco de Portugal, except 1960-63, own
estimates of trade of Metropolitan Portugal with
overseas territories. 1975-79 Banco de Portugal,
Boletim Trimestral (78-79 values are preliminary).

Same deflator as in Chart 4-1.

the preference of the Central Bank for gold
reserves.[48] Therefore, despite the brutal decline
in the foreign asset position in 1974-77, over
half of the Bank of Portugal's reserves are still
in gold, which, valued at the free market price
was 10 percent higher than the total foreign
liabilities of the public sector at year-end, and
had recovered to 25 percent higher by mid 1979.[49]
In fact, the 688 tons of gold held by the Banco de
Portugal at year end were worth more than $11
billion at the London price of gold, and they were
valued at $1 billion.[50]

6. THE REAL WAGE AND INCOME DISTRIBUTION

From the mid-fifties to 1970, there was a
steady increase in the real wage in manufacturing
in the Lisbon area, the trend in which, depicted
in Chart 4.3, can be taken as a rough indicator of
the marginal value product of labor relative to the
price of the consumer basket[51]. Increasing demand
for labor during the import-substitution growth of
the fifties continued when the association with
EFTA generated the process of export-led growth. In
the sixties this process was sustained by reduced
supply due to increasing migration[52].

Furthermore, rural migration went directly out
of the country, rather than first to the city, as
was the case in Greece and Spain[53], so that unemployment was low in agriculture as well as in
manufacturing.

In part as a consequence of continued excess
demand for labor, the corporatist institutions
designed in the thirties to fight unemployment
became unable to respond to workers' needs in an
effective way, thus leading to some clandestine
attempts at trade unionization. Increased tourism,
in particular by emigrants, on the other hand, had
a demonstration effect in creating or reinforcing
a trade-unionist attitude in the industrial working
class.

In the early seventies, as the stock market
was experiencing a speculative boom, industrial
concentration was reaching a "European" scale and
labor productivity was growing at over 10 percent
per annum, inflation and wage controls led to a
stagnation, and maybe even a small decline, of the
real wage, as shown in the Chart.[54] On the other
hand, the protracted war effort overseas, a
political issue since the 1969 elections, was

CHART 4-3
REAL WAGE INDICES

1973 = 100

Sources: Solid line 1957-78. Daily wages in manufacturing
and transportation in Lisbon divided by the Lisbon
consumer price index, including rent, from INE,
Boletim Mensal de Estatistica, as reported in IFS.
(1957-1960 nominal wage from European Historical
Statistics). Both indices are unavailable for
1979.

Broken line 1973-79. Total earnings in manufacturing divided by the new Continental consumer
price index excluding rent from Banco de Portugal,
Boletim Trimestral (nominal earnings growth in
1979; 4 taken to be at the 20% ceiling lifted in
December).

becoming increasingly divisive, even within the
Armed Forces.

In 1973, civilian opposition to the government
was exacerbated by the poor harvest and, above all,
the dramatic oil embargo, while adverse military
developments in the Guinea front threatened to
bring about a confrontation between the government
and the Army.

The situation deteriorated sharply in early
1974 and, as the world economy was sliding into
the deepest postwar recession, the "Armed Forces
Movement" staged a swift and bloodless coup on
April 25.

The civilian opposition to the old regime, the
only organized core of which proved to be the Communist Party, was thus brought to power. Wage
policy became more and more divorced from market
considerations, so that nominal wages took an upward jump and, as inflationary expectations were
temporarily reversed, real wages increased substantially. Interestingly, militant wage increases
were often brought about by far-left unions, against
the recommendations of Communist leaders. In any
event, as shown in the Chart, the increase in total
labor costs was even larger, and accelerated in
1975, even though the price index used to deflate
annual earnings excludes controlled rent and therefore also increased faster than the one used to
deflate daily wages.

The difference is, however, not crucial to
the "relative deprivation" story of the Portuguese
Revolution suggested by the inverted J pattern of
the real wage in the antecedent years.[55] This story
helps to explain how a seemingly reformist military
coup precipitated into the "Lisbon Commune" of mid-
1975 before returning to its initial vocation after
the failure of the November 25 coup. It would be
difficult to imagine such a wage policy if the
bureautically planned economy advocated by the
organized core would not have been entirely by-
passed by anarchaic but initially successful
attempts of consumers to increase their living
standards.

There is conflicting evidence on whether the
sharp decline in the real wage began in 1976 (solid
line in the chart) or in 1977 (broken line). The
latter picture emerges from looking at the labor
share in national income, but similar caveats about
the poor quality of the data have to be borne in
mind. Thus, the percentage of net national income
at factor cost going to labor, including employers'

Social Security payments, increased by 15 percentage
points from 1973 to 1975 and stayed constant in
1976. However, it dropped by 10 percentage points
from 1976 to 1978,[56] the same order of magnitude
of the drop in the daily real wage.

So, while it is clear that the equilibrium real
wage has fallen[57], it is not clear from the Chart
whether actual wages are at the 1973 or at the 1966
level, an emotionally and politically important
issue.

Furthermore, the increase in the progressivity
of wage taxation was also quite drastic. Between
1973 and 1977, nominal before tax wages would have
to double for lower income and be multiplied five
fold for higher income so as to preserve after tax
purchasing power over domestic goods; and the
factors would become five and eleven respectively
for purchasing power over U.S. goods.[58]

That the fall in real wages could have been
such a central feature of an adjustment process
largely conducted by "pro-labor" governments may
be explained by workers perceiving that most of the
post-revolutionary increases could not be but
temporary and thus adjusting expectations downward
substantially. Nevertheless, it is probable that
some money and exchange rate illusion on the part
of workers has also been present.

The decline in absolute living standards can
be related to evidence on the size distribution of
income showing that at base period prices the middle range increased its share from 35 percent to
60 percent between 1968 and 1977 (see Table 4.9).
At 1973-74 prices the increase in that same range
is from 42 percent to 52 percent, whereas the
three highest brackets increase from 8 percent to
37 percent in the same period.

In short, the fact that personal distribution
of income in Portugal is more equitable made it
easier to accept that the standard of living of
the workers, in particular skilled workers, would
have declined relative to the early seventies,
immediately after the across the board increases
of 1974-75.

7. IMPLICATIONS OF STRUCTURAL INTERDEPENDENCE

In the literature of the fifties and sixties,
political integration--in the sense of the establishment of a security community--was approached
as an "incremental" result of the dismantling of

184

TABLE 4.9
Size Distribution of Income (%)

Monthly Income in Dollars	In 1967/68 Prices			In 1973/74
	67/68	73/74	77	77
65	60.0	50.1	33.2	11.9
65-130	28.3	33.5	39.3	29.0
130-196	6.9	8.5	20.1	22.8
196-261				18.6
261-392	4.8	7.9	7.4	14.0
392				3.7

Source: Expresso n. 337 of 4/12/79 p. 4-5R with
data from INE, Inquérito às Receitas e Despesas
Familiares, 1977 and for 1977 estimates of Ministerio da Habitação e Obras Publicas converted into
dollars at $1 = 38.277.

national barriers to the movements of goods and
factors of production between countries characterized structurally by economic interdependence and
socio-cultural homogeneity and behaviorally by
mutual political responsiveness.[59] The quantitative
variant of this approach is thus mostly concerned
with the identification of, and correlation among,
attributes of various countries with respect to the
structural dimensions, supplementing the analysis
with measures of mutual political responsiveness
such as patterns of U.N. voting and membership in
international organizations.[60]

The attributes are then reduced to a few
orthogonal factors which operationalize the main
dimensions of structural homogeneity. For example,
using as factors "economic development", "Communism", "intensive agriculture", and "Catholic culture",[61] the world in the late 50's was divided into
four geographically well-defined regions, Afro-Asia,
Western Community, Latin America, and Eastern
Europe, and a group of "semi-developed Latins"
including Spain, Portugal, Chile, Uruguay, Puerto
Rico, and Cuba, halfway between the Western Community and Latin America.[62]

The "region" where Portugal is integrated
according to these results, has interesting implications for the idea of Iberian unity, historically
attempted by military or doctrinal means but systematically resisted by the population.[63] Naturally, the factors chosen are not able to capture the
"Western Community" dimension that the policies of
Portugal in the African territories and with respect to Brazil were taken to have in the idiosyn-
cracies of the rulers of the time. But they do
suggest indirectly the major change brought about
by the membership in EFTA in 1960 and the growth of
labor migration toward the EEC by giving a measure
of the original distance between Portugal and
Europe.[64]

Another major change, relating to the behavioral variable as measured, refers to voting
alignment in the United Nations, which changed
dramatically when the issue of self-determination
became central--and Portugal was candidate for
membership of the Security Council.[65] The only
political link to the Western Community in terms of
membership in regional organizations was then to be
the North Atlantic Treaty Organization.

Indeed, the participation of Portugal in the
international economic institutions that emerged
in the post-war period was a cautious one. Portugal

was a founding member of the Organization for
European Economic Cooperation and the European
Payments Union in 1948 but it only participated in
the Marshall Plan in 1950. Having become a founding member of the Organization for European Cooperation and Development, she joined the European Monetary Agreement in 1958. In 1961, soon after EFTA
was created she joined the World Bank and the
International Monetary Fund.[66]

The membership of EFTA took place in the
particularly favorable conditions set out in the G
Annex to the Treaty of Stockholm. As the main
partner of EFTA, the United Kingdom, prepared to
join the EEC, Portugal signed a free trade agreement with the EEC in May 1972, while remaining in
the mini-EFTA to the present. With the 1974 Revolution the intention was expressed to expand the
1972 Agreement in view of joining the EEC, since
the political obstacles to membership had disappeared.

The process was delayed by Portugal's domestic
troubles and only in November of 1975 did the
European Investment Bank approve an emergency loan
to Portugal, which was incorporated in the June
1976 Additional Protocol to the 1972 Agreement.
This implied in particular that the calendar for
dismantling of Portuguese tariffs on industrial
products was postponed from 1980 to 1985 while the
complete elimination of EEC tariffs was anticipated
from 1977 to 1976 and new tariffs on infant industries could be levied until 1981. The agreement
is, however, not applicable to "sensitive" industrial products and to transformed agricultural
products.[67]

In March 1977 the Portuguese government formally applied for full membership in the EEC and the
European Commission advised the Council to accept
in April 1978. Negotiations opened formally in
October 1978 but problems of bureaucratic politics
on the Portuguese side delayed progress until the
Spring of 1979.[68]

The slow progress in the negotiations, in
comparison for instance with Spain, may be one
factor explaining the attitude of ignorance about
the EEC that is evident from the responses in the
top panel of Table 4.10. Even though survey data
are to be handled with care, and a comparison with
evidence from other applicants, or even members,
would not reveal a much greater knowledge, a percentage of over half of the population of the two
largest cities suggests a very high national

average indeed.

Another striking feature of the Table refers, instead, to those who know what the Common Market is. In effect, a clear distinction appears between the residents of the coastal cities of Lisbon and Porto who take the view that membership will make life worse with respect to crime and cost of living, and the cities of the interior, Beja in the South and Guarda in the North, where the opposite belief is expressed. The industrial city of Leiria-- North of Lisbon--falls in between since the cost of living is expected to decline. With respect to taxes, furthermore, an increase is expected by everybody, particularly in Leiria and Lisbon. In turn, the issue of "Agrarian Reform" is believed to become "worse" in Lisbon and neighboring Leiria but not in the "red capital" of Beja, where incidentally unemployment is also believed to improve. Another interesting aspect of the responses is that there is an across the board belief that the "economic crisis"--a staple in the political vocabulary--will improve.

Overall, the responses would suggest that European integration, while ignored in its institutional underpinnings, is taken as given by the urban population who tends to consider it a step in solving the "economic crisis". This may be related to the suggestion made in the previous section, that the attitude of the population toward the government changed dramatically with the perceived change in late 1973-early 1974 in the trade-off between economic prosperity and political freedom. Similarly, the disappointment of the euphoria of the Revolution, which seems to be pervasive in Portugal at the moment--and would be easy to infer from the brutal drop in real wages-- was probably important in shaping the attitudes toward the European Community revealed by Table 4.10. Indeed, it may well have been more important, not only than the reduced media coverage of the negotiation process but also, for that matter, than the channels of structural interdependence of the early seventies.

This is another way of saying that there is increasing awareness of the implications of policy interdependence.[69] Aside from the serious requirements of fiscal harmonization, particularly the introduction of a direct tax on overall income and a value added tax, economic integration has strong implications on the effectiveness of the instruments of macro-economic stabilization policy. Even

TABLE 4.10
Attitudes Towards the EC

Question: Do you know what the Common Market is?

	Lisbon (MET)	Porto (MET)	Beja	Leiria	Guarda
No	49	54	56	34	53
Yes but cannot define	-	19	27	19	-
Yes and define	51	28	17	47	47

Question: Will the entrance in the Common Market make your life better or worse?

	Lisbon (MET)		Porto (MET)		Beja		Leiria		Guarda	
	Better	Worse	Better	Worse	Better	Worse	Better	Worse	Better	Worse
Cost of living	32	42	19	30	52	30	48	37	35	13
Education	23	21	20	11	33	18	16	25	26	7
Agrarian reform	22	34	17	16	34	28	19	49	20	14
Housing	21	24	18	18	33	19	38	38	24	9
Unemployment	32	32	22	23	53	31	68	22	28	14
Crime	14	26	14	24	24	22	10	37	18	11

| Economic Crisis | 44 | 33 | 22 | 20 | 47 | 28 | 68 | 30 | 43 | 16 |
| Taxes | 18 | 37 | 11 | 32 | 19 | 26 | 19 | 63 | 15 | 21 |

Source: Expresso n° 303, August 11, 1979. Survey conducted by CONTAGEM with a sample of 1200 (600 in Metropolitan Lisbon, 200 in Metropolitan Porto and 400 in the three provincial cities).

after the economic liberalization the last years of
the earlier regime, administrative controls remained
the preferred policy instrument and were supple-
mented after April 25 by the extinction of emerging
capital markets and the drastic expansion of the
public sector that culminated in the nationalizations of 1975. It was not until the stabilization
program agreed upon with the IMF in mid-1978 that
a greater reliance was placed on market mechanisms.
The spectacular recovery of exports and remittances
in 1978-79 allows some optimism about the effectiveness of these signals, but they will certainly
not be enough to solve the formidable twin problems
of short term stabilization and long run growth.
While the analysis of these problems is beyond
the scope of this paper, the objective of stabilization does introduce a new dimension in the
optimality of European integration, having to do
with public rather than private goods. It has been
shown that the optimum size of the integrated area
differs sharply for these two types of goods;
whereas technological forces lead to a large optimal area for private goods (in the limit the world),
different preferences for the provision of public
goods, in particular across cultural boundaries,
point to a much smaller optimal area there.[70]

The deterioration of the international environment acquires then an added relevance, insofar as
the increased "turbulence" has effects on the
decision making process. Even if these effects are
not such as to lead to the abandonment of the
"incrementalist rationality",[71] the new tradeoff
between political and economic aspects of the
Second Enlargement in general, and of the accession
of Portugal to the EEC in particular, can certainly
be seen as counter-examples to traditional "political integration" theory. And it is puzzling that
this issue be conspicuously absent from the usual
professional <u>fora</u>.

8.   CONCLUSIONS

A few years ago, Portugal was advertised to
English speaking tourists as "Europe's best kept
secret." Turning the slogan around, one might say
that the consequences of European integration have
been Portugal's best kept secret. Despite electoral pledges about Europe's stake in Portuguese
democracy, most people do not seem to even know
what the Common Market is.

True, beyond presenting membership in the
European Community as a natural consequence of the
passing of the "imperial cycle" of the nation's
history, post revolutionary governments gave little
systematic attention to the problem. A very recent
statement of European intent notwithstanding, the
political establishment has been attempting to
find a workable compromise between the hopes of
April 25 and the realities of twelve governments
in six years. The increased population is adjusting to a painful decline in living conditions and
the "animal spirits" of the remaining entrepreneurs
are still affected by the overhang of the massive
nationalizations of 1975 and of the irregular en-
forcement of the laws of agrarian reform. Concern
over short run macroeconomic stabilization objectives has recently been competing with electoral
politics, with detrimental consequences for the
long run growth prospects of the territory.

This paper argued that, whereas Portugal can
probably expect to receive some real development
resources from the Community, it is quite mistaken
to believe that the economic consequences of joining the EEC will be the financing by the Community
of the remains of "Portuguese democratic socialism."
In fact, even if the Twelve restore overall cohesion and growth, structural interdependence alone
is not likely to support the process of autonomous
economic development which is essential for European integration not to lead to national disintegration.

When the prospects of increased interdependence are interpreted in this light, passivity in
the negotiations becomes a dangerous "laissez
faire" substitute for the traditional Portuguese
caution in dealing with her powerful neighbors.

NOTES

1. Kindleberger, op.cit., p. 191. This he calls "cultural pluralism" and contrasts it with the traditional notions of "melting pot and assimilation".

2. This is well documented in B. Balassa, editor, European Economic Integration, Amsterdam: North Holland, 1975, particularly p. 108 ff. See also our review; "Vinte anos de integração económica europeia," Economia, Vol. 1, No. 2, May 1977, p. 369-373.

3. P. Krugman, Intraindustry Specialization and the Gains from Trade, mimeo, MIT, August 1979, has a model of the transition from Hecksheer-Ohlin to intraindustry trade which brings out Balassa's early findings, reviewed in op. cit.

4. The dependence/interdependence controversy is explored in J. Macedo, Interdependencia Económica, Sistema Monetário Internacional e Integração Portuguesa, Banco de Fomento Nacional Estudos, 12, Lisbon, 1977, part I.

5. See European Communities - Commission, Economic and Sectoral Commission Analyses supplementing its views on enlargement, Supplement 3/78 to Bulletin of EC, n°48 (emphasis in the original).

6. Ibid. n° 48.

7. Ibid., No. 71. The productivity figures are from T. Josling, Problems for the Common Agricultural Policy of an Enlarged European Community, paper presented at the Conference on Portugal and the Enlargement of the European Community, organized by Inteuropa and the Trade Policy Research Centre, January 1980, hereafter referred to as Inteuropa. See also L. Katseli-Papaefstratiou, "Enlargement of the European Community and the Common Agricultural Policy", Economic Growth Center Discussion Paper No. 301, Yale University, November 1978.

8. See Kindleberger, op. cit., for this application of the Lewis model.

9. See, for instance, C. Palloix, L'economie mondiale capitaliste, Paris: Maspero, 1968. A similar result in a Hecksheer-Ohlin model with increasing returns to scale is presented in P. Krugman, "Trade, Accumulation and Uneven Development", Economic Growth Center Discussion Paper No. 311, Yale University, May 1979.

10. See B. Balassa, op.cit., p. 258 ff. for further evidence.

11. See J. Macedo, "O'Triangulo Dourado' da CEE", Suplemento "Economia e Finanças", Diário de

Noticias, 10/10/73 reproduced in "Interdependencia Economica e Dependencia Externa. Textos Praticos", mimeo, Catholic University of Portugal, 1975.

12. See T. Swan, "Economic Control in a Dependent Economy," Economic Record, March 1960, p. 51-66 and P. Kouri, Profitability and Growth in a Small Open Economy, in A. Lindbeck, editor, Inflation and Unemployment in Small Open Economies, Amsterdam: North-Holland, 1979, p. 129-142.

13. This expression was introduced by R. Cooper, The Economics of Interdependence, New York: McGraw Hill, 1968 who used the example of Belgium in the original Six. The original idea goes back to A. Hirschmann, National Power and the Structure of Foreign Trade, Berkeley, 1945.

14. Using revised productivity data from Banco de Portugal for 1974 and 1975 the average is 5.1 percent p.a.

15. This emphasis is shared by B. Balassa, Portugal in Face of the Common Market, paper presented at the Second International Conference on the Portuguese Economy in September 1979, hereafter referred to as Gulbenkian 1979.

16. See S. Kuznets, Economic Growth of Nations, Harvard, 1971, p. 231 and H. Chenery, Structural Change and Development Policy, Oxford, 1979, p. 18. Lobao, op. cit., Table 4, p. 189 reports agricultural labor productivity relative to total which fell from 57 percent in 1960 to 51 percent in 1970 and 39 percent in 1976.

17. It was 7.7 percent in 1963, 8.8 percent in 1968; 10.8 percent in 1973 and 7.6 percent in 1974. See World Bank, Agriculture.

18. See R. Amaro, "A agricultura portuguesa e a integração europeia: a experience do passado (EFTA) e a perspectiva do futuro (CEE)", Análise Social, Vol. 14, 1978, 2, p. 278-310.

19. The share of petroleum imports in the trade deficit, 20 percent in 1973, was over 30 percent in 1977 and 1978.

20. Accordingly, there has been considerable debate amongst agricultural economists about the consequences of Agrarian Reform. A noted instance is the comment of J. Espada to the paper of F. Estacio and A. Egbert, "O Sector Agricola em Portugal: Caracterização e Medidas de Politica", in The German Marshall Fund and the Gulbenkian Foundation (sponsors), Conferencia Internacional sobre Economia Portuguesa, Lisbon, 1977, hereafter referred to as Gulbenkian 1977, p. 103-151, assessed in Economia, January 1977, pages 159-162. A

passionate description of the process can be found
in A. Estrela, "A Reform Agrária Portuguesa,"
Análise Social, n° 54, 1978, 2, p. 237-252.
   21. Representing 72.3 percent of the UCP area
and 81 percent of employment in UCP's. See World
Bank, Agriculture, cit.
   22. Data from Heimpel, "The Cooperation of the
EC with Southern Europe: Some Problems in the
Integration of Portugal's Agriculture into the
Common Market" in Gulbenkian, 1977, cit., pages
253-257. See also Lobao, op. cit.
   23. See E. Thorbecke and E. Pagoulatos, "The
effects of European economic integration on agriculture" in Balassa, European, cit., page 306. See
also Jossling, op. cit.
   24. See Katseli, op. cit., page 6.
   25. See H. Kim, Agricultural Prices and Subsidies - Portugal Case Study, World Bank mimeo, 1978.
   26. Exports and Imports fob as a proportion
of gdp in market prices from IFS. Trends in the
60's and early 70's are discussed in Macedo, Interdependencia, cit., p. 271 ff.
   27. These percentages are based on figures in
1970 prices derived at the World Bank. They probably underestimate the full contribution of export
growth because they exclude indirect effects.
   28. In 1974-76 the average share of consumption
goods in exports was 38 percent and 16 percent in
imports. The figure for intermediate goods were
51 percent and 62 percent, respectively, and for
investment goods 11 percent and 21 percent, respectively. See J. Toscano, Avaliação economica de
projectos segundo a metodologia do Banco Mundial,
Banco de Fomento Nacional Estudos 14, Lisbon, 1978,
p. 54 with data from INE, Estatisticas do Comércio
Externo, Vol. II.
   29. These figures were obtained from the 1970
input-output matrix normalized to match the 1975
figures for imports. The import content of exports
was 33.5 percent. See Abel et al., op. cit., p.
79. Without the normalization the import content
of investment and exports drop to 35 percent and
25 percent respectively. It is therefore likely
that the figures from the 1974 matrix would be
higher than the ones quoted in the text.
   30. The numbers presented are the natural logs
multiplied by 100 of the ratio a_i^x/a_i^m where
$a_i^z = z_i/\Sigma_i z_i$ (and $Z = X,M$) is the share of commodity i. More complex indicators can be found in
B. Balassa, "Trade Liberalization and 'Revealed'
Comparative Advantage", The Manchester School of

Economic and Social Studies, Vol. 33, No. 2, 1965,
p. 99-123 and "'Revealed' Comparative Advantage
Revisited: An Analysis of Relative Export Shares
of the Industrial Countries, 1953-1971", ibid.,
Vol. 45, No. 4, 1977, pages 327-44. The values
reported in Table 4.10 were taken from J. Donges
and K.W. Schatz, Growth and Trade Aspects of the
Proposed Enlargement of the European Community,
Kieler Arbeitspapier No. 79, Kiel Institute of
World Economics, October 1978, Table 7, page 18.
    31. See figures for 1960 and 1970 in Donges-
Schatz, op.cit.
    32. See other comparative evidence on this
point in J. Donges and K.W. Schatz, "Competitiveness and Growth Prospects in an Enlarged European
Community," *The World Economy*, May 1979, pages 213-
228 (abbreviated version of op.cit.) and in R.
Eckhaus, Development Strategies and the International Division of Work, in Gulbenkian, 1979, cit.
    33. In 1975 the proportion of foreign direct
investment to the current account was 5 percent
both in Portugal and Spain (less than 1 percent for
Greece) whereas the proportion of total private
capital was 2.3 percent for Portugal and almost 34
percent for Spain. See Banco de Portugal 1977
Report, page 131.
    34. See J. Macedo, Foreign Direct Investment in
Metropolitan Portugal: A legal and economic analysis, unpublished manuscript, Yale University,
June, 1972 adapted in Interdependencia, op.cit.,
p. 291.
    35. See J. Donges, Foreign Investment in Portu-
gal, in Gulbenkian 1979. The Institute of Foreign
Investment warns however that stock data are quite
unreliable. See IIE, Investmento Estrangeiro em
Portugal 1978/79, mimeo, 1980.
    36. The restrictive foreign investment code of
1976 has been replaced by a more attractive regime.
See J. Leitão, "O Investimento Estrangeiro na
Estrategia de Desenvolvimento da Economia Portuguesa. Alguns aspectos jurídicos e de política
legislativa", in Confederação da Industria Portuguesa, I Congresso das Actividades Economicas, Vol.
I, Lisbon, 1979, pages 59-72.
    37. See J. Macedo, loc. cit., using data from
the Luso-German Chamber of Commerce. For further
evidence see M.B. Martins, Multinacionais em Portugal, Lisbon: Estampa, 1975 and L.S. Matos, Investi-
mentos estrangeiros em Portugal, Lisboa: Seara
Nova, 1972.
    38. See J. Donges, op.cit., p. 12 who uses

discriminant analysis for this purpose.
39. The figures for workers migration include clandestine emigration and are taken from M. Barbosa, Growth Migration and the Balance of Payments in a Small Open Economy, unpublished Ph.D. Thesis, Yale University, 1977, p. 206, series (3). Some alternative estimates for the 1970's are:

	(1)	(2)	(3)	(4)	(5)	(6)
1970	110.5	168.	n.a.	179	n.a.	-149
1	80.3	139.	n.a.	150	n.a.	n.a.
2	44.2	94.	n.a.	105	n.a.	n.a.
3	64.2	110.	85.0	120	80.0	- 72
4	23.9	64.	23.0	70	43.0	165
5	9.0	35.	7.0	40	25.0	336
6	n.a.	n.a.	n.a.	35	17.0	- 24
7	n.a.	n.a.	n.a.	n.a.	17.0	n.a.

(1) Net emigration of workers from L. Taylor, "A balanca de pagamentos portuguesa" in Gulbenkian, 1977, op.cit., pages 283-317.
(2) Total emigration, (3) Emigration of active population both from J. Moura, "Problemas e Politicas de Emprego no Continente", ibid., page 517-577.
(4) same as (3) from the 1974 Report of the Banco de Portugal, which specifies that the origin is the Secretaria de Estado do Emprego. These figures are close to the ones reported in Portugal: Current and Economic Trends, World Bank Country Study, November 1978, the OECD 1974 Survey.
(5) Same as (3) from Banco de Portugal 1977 Annual Report.
(6) Net migration, 1974 and 1975 reflecting returnees from World Bank.
40. M. Barbosa, op.cit., page 204 computed the foreign wage from real earning rates in France, Germany, U.S. and Canada with weights the proportion of the emigrant labor force in 1955 and 1970-73. Using 1963 exchange rates he arrived for 1972 at the figure of 84.8 thousand 1963 escudos per man-year whereas for Portugal the figure was 4.1 thousand. B. Balassa, "Industrial and Trade Policy in Portugal", in Gulbenkian, 1977, p. 236 quotes figures for industrial wages in Portugal in 1975 as being one-third of what they were in France and two-fifths of what they were in Germany.
41. See J. Macedo, op. cit. on note 58 below, p. 195 and 323. The quarterly index of real wages with base 1973; 1=1 computed relative to a weighted average of France, Germany, U.K. and U.S., with weights given by average current account shares in 1973-77. Including relative productivity smooths the series somewhat, see Ibid.

42. In fact if emigration is viewed as a dis-equilibrium phenomenon, steady-state in an economy with endogenous migration requires remittances to exist and be at least partly saved. See J. Macedo, "Emigration and Remittances in Neoclassical Steady-State", Economia, Vol. 1, No. 1, January 1977, pages 95-111. M. Barbosa, "Emigration Without Remittan-ces: a comment", ibid., Vol. 1, No. 3, October 1977 has shown that this does not hold if emigra-tion is proportional to the non-migrant--rather than the total-labor force and emigration is therefore a steady state phenomenon. In Growth, Migration . . ., op. cit., page 25, he shows that this is implied by the existence of a fixed factor like land when the rate of land-augmenting technical progress is different from the natural rate of growth. However, his basic model and the empirical results ibid., especially page 156, are inconsistent with steady-state emigration.

43. See comparative data in J. Macedo, Unre-quited transfers in an open economy, unpublished manuscript, Yale University, May 1972.

44. Data from M. Barbosa, Growth, Migration, op.cit., Table 4.1, page 77.

45. A related development was the decline in tourism, which recently has recovered enough to offset the increased outflow on the interest account.

46. For further detail on this framework and comparative data see J. Macedo, Unrequited, op.cit.

47. The figures are equal to the change in the stock of foreign assets of the banking system de-flated by the foreign price level less the capital losses due to foreign inflation.

48. For an historical overview of Portuguese economic development with particular reference to exchange rate policy see J. Macedo, "Portuguese currency experience: an historical perspective", in Estudos en Homenagem ao Prof. Doutor Teixeira, Vol. 2, special issue of Boletim da Faculdade de Direito de Coimbra, 1979.

49. See Banco de Portugal, Communique of 9/25/79.

50. The December average price of gold was $512 an ounce. In April 1980 gold was revalued at $255 dollars an ounce. 26 percent of the capital gain of $4.6 billion will make up a reserve fund for future losses due to changes in the price of gold or the exchange rate. The rest offsets the debt of the government to the central Bank.

51. Barbosa, op.cit., p. 107 estimated a CES

198

production function from 1953 to 1972 with capital,
labor and labor augmenting technical change for the
Portuguese economy and obtained the real wage by
adjusting the product wage (marginal value product
of labor) with the consumer price index. The
picture is roughly the same as in Chart 4.1, but the
absolute value of the actual real wage during the
period of estimation was much higher than the
marginal product of labor. Using data on the functional distribution of income from 1965 to 1972 he
concludes that the average ratio was 4.2 (see ibid.,
p. 142, footnote 7).

52. Barbosa, op.cit., p. 152 and figure 5.3
shows that labor supply was increasing until 1962.

53. See evidence in C. Kindleberger, op. cit.,
p. 105.

54. Even though the marginal value product of
labor did not fall, Barbosa estimates show a 1 percent decline in the real wage in 1971. See op.cit.,
p. 209, series (29).

55. See J. Davies, "Toward a Theory of Revolu-
tion", American Sociological Review, Vol. 27, No. 1,
February 1962, p. 5-20 and T. Gurr, Why Men Rebel,
Princeton University Press, 1970.

56. The figures reported by O.E. Carvalho and
M.L. Nunes, Aspectos da Distribuição dos Rendimen-
tos em Portugal no periodo 1973-1978, in Gulbenkian
1979 are 1, in percent:

1973   1974   1975   1976   1977   1978
51.6   56.9   69.3   68.7   59.6   57.4

where the 1977 and 1978 values are estimates using
wage inflation ceilings of 15 percent and 20 percent
respectively. The levels are substantially lower
than the ones inferred from the estimates of the
share of labor in production costs in construction
and manufacturing, which are considered more reliable, but the changes reported in the text are
roughly similar. Note that the figures reported in
Departamento Central de Planeamento, Situacao Economica Portuguesa, Mimeo., May 1976; in A. Abel, L.
Beleza, J. Frankel, R. Hill e P. Krugman, "A Economia Portuguesa: Evolução Recente e Situação
Actual", in Gulbenkian 1977, p. 31-91, for 1973-
1975 and in World Bank Country Study, cit., for
1973-77 are different again.

57. The decline from 1973 to 1978 comes close
to the one of the daily real wage in the Chart.
See P. Krugman and J. Macedo, "The Economic Consequences of the April 25th Revolution", Economic
Growth Center Discussion Paper No. 326, Yale University, November 1979, Chapter 2 in this volume.

58. Using the numbers computed by M. Cadilhe
and A. Costa. "Remunerações, Inflação e Fiscalidade em Portugal: 1973 e 1977", Economia, Vol. II,
No. 2., May 1978, p. 297-306, and the change in the
purchasing power of the escudos in terms of U.S.
goods from J. Macedo, Portfolio Diversification and
Currency Inconvertibility: Three Essays in International Monetary Economics, unpublished Ph.D.
Thesis, Yale University, 1979. More specifically,
the numbers are as follows:

1973		1977	
"contos"/month	base	domestic	U.S.
5	1	2.40	5.08
20	1	2.95	6.26
40	1	5.45	11.56

See further evidence in P. Krugman and J. Macedo,
op.cit., Table 8, page 28.

59. See in particular K. Deutsch et.al., Political Community and the North Atlantic Area: International Organization in the Light of Historical
Experience, Princeton: Princeton University Press,
1957; E. Haas, The Uniting of Europe: Political,
Social and Economic Forces, 1950-57, Stanford:
Stanford University Press, 1958 and B. Balassa, The
Theory of Economic Integration, McGraw-Hill, 1961.
In "A policy for Portugal with respect to political
integration," unpublished manuscript, Yale University, January 1972, adapted in J. Macedo, Interdependencia, pages 331-347, we attempted to relate
the view of Deutsch of political integration as a
security community and the view of Cooper, op.cit.,
of economic integration as interdependence in the
construction of a rational choice for Portugal, and
then discussed bureaucratic politics and the
societal roots of foreign policy as alternative
approaches to the problem, in the spirit of the
analysis of G. Allison, Essence of Decision: Explaining the Cuban Missile Crisis, Boston: Little,
Brown, 1971. In a recent critique of "political
integration theory", E. Haas, "Turbulent Fields and
the Theory of Regional Integration", International
Organization, Vol. 30, Spring, 1976, pages 173-212,
points out that the analysis of "crisis" in international politics cannot be easily applied to the
integration process, even when "turbulent". Nevertheless, the contribution of Allison certainly goes
beyond the analysis of international "crisis", as
Haas acknowledges (Ibid., page 184 footnote 11 in
fine) when he refers to the "incremental bargaining
style of bureaucratic behavior" that is prominent
in Allison's bureaucratic model as it is in Haas'

early work quoted above.

60. See B. Russett, International Regions and the International System: A Study in Political Ecology, Chicago: Rand McNally, 1967 for an analysis of 82 countries along these lines.

61. The factors are obtained from 29 variables which show a correlation of .6 or higher on the four dimensions mentioned. The main ones are GNP per capita (.94), newspapers per capita (.93) and share of non-agricultural workers in employment (.93) for factor one; Communist votes as percent of all votes (.96), central government expenditure as percent of GNP (.95) and ditto for revenue (.94) for factor two; population density (.9) for factor three and Roman Catholics as percent of population (.87) for factor four. See the discussion in Russett, ibid. and also Macedo, Interdependencia, cit., page 336.

62. Having quoted "L'Afrique commence aux Pyrenees" on page 1, the proximity of Iberia to Latin America leads Russett to add parenthetically that "the French proverb should be revised to declare, 'Latin America begins at the Pyrenees'" (op. cit., page 34). Haiti, Jamaica, Guyana, South Africa, and China were dubbed "unclassifiable."

63. See Borges de Macedo, As condições da esperanca, Lisbon, 1978, page 16 and Uma perspectiva, op.cit.

64. The political implications of this structural change for Southern Europe are emphasized by J. Linz, "Europe's Southern Frontier: Evolving Trend Towards What?", Daedalus, Winter 1979, page 17.

65. See Franco Nogueira, Ao Nações Unidas e Portugal, Lisbon, 1961.

66. On these developments see Macedo, Interdependencia, cit., page 303 ff, Portuguese Currency Experience, cit., and references therein. The conventional view emphasizes the isolationism rather than the caution of Portuguese foreign policy in the post-war period. A recent example is J. Cravinho, "Motives and Problems of the Second Enlargement: The Case of Portugal", paper presented at the Second Conference on Integration and Unequal Development, Madrid, Spain, October 1979. For instance, according to Cravinho, "Portuguese participation in EFTA was very clearly a choice for non commitment with European affairs" (page 9). Using measures of static integration effects by the EFTA Secretariat he goes on to downplay the structural effects of the EFTA induced export-led growth of

the sixties.

67. This is elaborated in Macedo, Interdependencia, cit., pages 348 ff. See also Pitta e Cunha, Portugal and the European Economic Community, paper presented at the II International Meeting on Modern Portugal, Durham, N.H., June 1979, forthcoming Economia.

68. Thus in late September a representative office of the European Commission was set up in Lisbon and in December a Complementary Protocol to the 1972 and 1976 Agreements was signed in Brussels. The document postpones tariff reductions on sensitive products and allows tariff increases on infant industries until 1982, and reduces the EEC quotas on paper and spirits but not on tomato concentrate, canned fish and table wines, see Expresso, no. 361, 9/29/79 and no. 373, 12/22/79.

69. A recent survey of the literature can be found in P. Kenen and P.R. Allen, Asset Markets, Exchange Rates and Economic Integration, Chapter 14, draft, Princeton University, July 1978, forthcoming, Cambridge University Press. The concept (so labelled by R. Bryant, Money and Monetary Policy in an Open Economy, Brookings, 1978, Chapter 9) has been popularized by R. Keohane and J. Nye, "International Interdependence and Integration," in F. Greenstein and N. Polsby (eds.), Handbook of Political Science, Vol. 8, Andover: Addison-Wesley, 1975, pages 363-414, who cite earlier hints in the international relations literature. It is further elaborated in R. Keohane and J. Nye, Power and Interdependence: World Politics in Transition, Little, Brown, 1977.

70. See R. Cooper, "Worldwide vs. regional economic integration: is there an optimal size of the integrated area?", Economic Growth Center Discussion Paper No. 220, Yale University, November 1974 and J. Macedo, Teoria da Integração Econômica, mimeo, Catholic University of Portugal, 1976.

71. According to E. Haas, op.cit., in favor of "a new decision-making rationality labelled 'fragmented issue linkage'-(. . .) suggesting that efforts are being made to cope with 'turbulence' in the industrial environment so as to avoid piecemeal solutions".

APPENDIX TABLE
SITC Categories Cited

03	Fish and fish preparation
05	Fruits and vegetables
1121	Wine of fresh grapes
24	Wood, lumber and cork
51	Chemical elements and compounds
52	Mineral tar and crude chemicals from coal, petroleum and natural gas
53	Dyeing, tanning and coloring products
54	Medical and pharmaceutical products
55	Essential oils and perfume materials, etc.
56	Fertilizers, manufactured
57	Explosives and pyrotechnic projects
58	Plastic materials, regenerated cellulose and artificial resin
59	Chemical materials and products, n.e.s.
61	Leather, leather manufactures, n.e.s.
62	Rubber manufactures, n.e.s.
63	Wood and cork manufactures (excl. furniture)
64	Paper, paperboard and manufactures thereof
65	Textile yarn, fabrics, made up articles and related products
66	Non-metallic mineral manufactures, n.e.s.
67	Iron and steel
68	Non-ferrous metal
69	Manufactures, n.e.s.
71	Machinery, other than electric
73	Transport equipment
81	Sanitary plumbing, heating, and lighting fixtures and fittings
82	Furniture
83	Travel goods, handbags and similar articles
84	Clothing
85	Footwear
86	Professional scientific and controlling instruments, watches and clocks
89	Miscellaneous manufactures, n.e.s.

COMMENT

Hans Schmitt

1. Braga de Macedo provides a wealth of information on the international transactions of
Portugal as they relate to the prospects of economic
and political integration with the European Community. He concludes that "autonomous economic
development is essential for European integration
not to lead to national disintegration." I shall
try to extract from his paper some of its more
controversial propositions, and by giving them
perhaps somewhat more precise expression, to
present in their sharpest form the issues raised
by him.

2. For Macedo economic integration is defined
by increasing interdependence. The process had
gained considerable momentum well before the revolution of April 25, 1974. In the first instance,
the proportion in gross domestic product of exports
of goods and nonfactor services rose from 18 per
cent in 1963 to 26 per cent in 1973. Within the
total of commodity exports, moreover, the proportion going to the nine countries of the European
Community increased from 37 per cent to 49 per
cent between the same years. Such exports can
therefore be regarded as having been the leading
sector in the rapid growth of the pre-revolutionary
economy.

Substantial integration took place in
factor markets as well as in product markets. As
Macedo notes, autonomous capital inflows particularly of direct investment gained in importance
over this period. Of even more decisive significance, however, was the phenomenal growth in labor
migration. By 1973, some 14 per cent of the combined Portuguese labor force were employed in the
European Community leaving less than 2 per cent
unemployed at home. Proceeding at a rate of over

100,000 per annum, net migration abroad absorbed
all the annual increment to the population of
working age in the pre-revolutionary period.
 The possibility of emigrating to better
paying jobs in the European Community put upward
pressure on Portuguese wages and consumption
standards. These could be accommodated without
jeopardizing the balance of payments by the rapidly
increasing return flows of emigrant remittances.
Remittances apart, the external deficit on goods
and nonfactor services rose in relation to gross
domestic product from 4.7 per cent in 1953, to 5.4
per cent in 1963 and 5.9 per cent in 1973. A much
faster rate of growth of wages would have required
cutbacks in investment and growth to keep that gap
from exceeding the finance available.
 Integration was thus a race between export
expansion and the wage increases that could have
retarded it by squeezing investment. To make
export-led growth possible, a large wage differential continued to be maintained between Portugal
and the European Community, even in the heyday of
emigration. This differential increased as real
wages first stagnated in 1970 and 1971, and then
even declined in 1972 and 1973. Set against the
increasingly powerful demonstration effect of
returning migrants, such relative deprivation was
in Macedo's view a major factor in setting the
stage for the revolution that followed in 1974.
 3. The Portuguese revolution spelled the collapse of an authoritarian regime that had over-
extended itself in colonial wars. Of equal
importance to its demise, Macedo suggests, was that
regime's unresponsiveness to wage pressures in a
labor market that had increasingly become integrated with the rest of Europe. Once this political barrier was removed real wages jumped--by 9 per
cent in the two years to 1975 if we take the Lisbon
wage index alone, by 14 per cent if we average it
with the same index for Oporto, and by 25 per cent
if we take annual earnings per man in manufacturing
for the country as a whole. The consequences were
predictable.
 To be sure, it was not only the increase
in wage costs that caused exports of goods and nonfactor services to drop 16 per cent in volume in
1974, and 16 per cent again in 1975. A fourfold
increase in world energy costs coincided with it,
and produced a recession in Portugal's major markets, including the European Community, that would
have slowed Portuguese exports in any case. There

was also a major loss of market shares, however.
And though interruptions in the productive process
may have been a factor at first, the loss of market
shares did not begin to be corrected until cost
competitiveness was later restored.

The catch-up in real wages also produced
a major shift in the distribution of income, raising the share of labor in the national income from
52 per cent in 1973 to 69 per cent in 1975.
Associated with it there was an increase in the
share of public and private consumption in domestic
expenditure from 87 per cent to 96 per cent. The
drop in the national savings rate exceeded con-
current decline in investment by a substantial
margin. Accordingly, the external deficit on goods
and nonfactor services doubled to 12 per cent of
gross domestic product in 1975, despite a fall in
the level of economic activity of perhaps 4 per
cent.

By reducing growth, excessive wage
increases reduced employment opportunities in
Portugal; the excess labor supply would normally
have been added to the flow of workers abroad.
However, in consequence of the energy-induced
recession in the rest of Europe, the flow of Portuguese emigrants to the European Community virtually
dried up. On top of this, the end of the colonial
wars in Africa brought a massive reflux of colo-
nists, which added at least 300,000 to the work
force in three years, and a minimum of 6 per cent
to the population as a whole. By 1975 unemployment
had jumped to at least 6 per cent, and may have
exceeded 10 per cent of the labor force.

Thus, just at the point when significant
increases in real wages were being realized, the
conditions for them had already disappeared. To
maintain the growth necessary to absorb the
increased labor force, while maintaining balance
of payments equilibrium, would have called for significant reductions rather than increases in real
wages. Such reductions were now to be achieved
through inflation. Real annual earnings per man in
manufacturing were cut 18 per cent from their 1975
highs, nearly back to their 1973 levels by 1978,
though the Lisbon wage index reported by Macedo
shows a more dramatic cutback to its mid-sixties
level.

4. The inflation that reduced real wages in
Portugal was accommodated by a progressive depre-
ciation of the exchange rate. As competitiveness
began to be restored, exports of goods and nonfactor

services recovered rapidly, growing in volume by 6
per cent in 1977 and by no less than 14 per cent in
1978. In relation to gross domestic product such
exports had dropped to about 17 per cent--in a
disastrous attempt to force growth in 1976 and 1977
on an uncompetitive base--but now rebounded to 20
per cent. Also, the share of commodity exports
going to the European Community increased to 56 per
cent in 1978, compared with 49 per cent in 1973.

Exports to the European Community have thus
resumed their role as the leading sector in Portuguese economic growth. Their momentum is likely in
future to be constrained by a shortage of capital
rather than of labor. To be sure, national savings
are beginning to recover as the share of wages in
income declines. Also, the massive flight of
capital that once threatened to make any significant
level of investment unsustainable, has now been
reversed by a drastic adjustment of interest rates
to more realistic levels. In addition, however,
Portuguese growth would also benefit from increased
access to foreign capital.

Instead of labor moving abroad in search
of capital, capital might in future come in to
employ labor at home. The focus in the integration
of factor markets would thus shift from labor markets to capital markets. To help facilitate this
development, at least in manufacturing, a number of
measures have already been taken. Thus the foreign
investment law has been revised to give greater
assurance to foreign investors, the scope of the
public and private sectors has been delimited by
law, the government has committed itself not to
undertake further nationalizations, and labor
legislation has been enacted to provide some limited
possibilities for layoffs of workers.

More capital, foreign and domestic, needs
also to be drawn into agriculture. As Macedo
points out, value added per head in Portuguese
agriculture remains barely above a quarter of the
European Community average despite a resource base
similar to that in Greece and Spain where it has
reached nearly one half. To help exploit this
potential a new agrarian reform law has established
the conditions under which land may be expropriated
in the South where production units are uneconomically large, while calling for the voluntary
consolidation of land holdings in the North where
they are uneconomically small.

5. The conclusion that emerges from this
analysis is that the economic integration of

Portugal with the European Community is no longer
an option but a fact. The question is how to
manage it. Macedo calls for autcnomous economic
development in Portugal to ensure that European
integration will not lead to national disintegration. An excessively rapid integration of labor
markets may well have threatened it, and a shift
to capital market integration may therefore be
preferable. The opportunities for managing it
democratically will be enhanced by full Portuguese
participation in the institutions of the Community.

COMMENT

Juergen B. Donges

     Portugal's entry into the European Community (EC) seems to be politically inevitable after the country has now satisfied the political conditions set forth by the Community. Perhaps as a result, the economic questions arising from the accession have been widely neglected in public discussion both in Portugal and in the EC countries. This paper rightly shows, however, that the economic implications can be rather subtle and complex.

     As I am much in agreement with what the author says, I shall extend his analysis somewhat and raise the following three questions: What is the potential impact of integration on Portugal's trade structure? Which growth effects can be expected? And how should Portugal reform its prevailing system of incentives, if it is to take full advantage of economic opportunities in an enlarged Community?

     In discussing the first question, I would draw a sharper distinction than Braga de Macedo does between the trade patterns of Portugal with the Community and those with third countries. Take for example agriculture: While exports which already go largely to the Common Market will not be in-fluenced much by the accession, imports will. One problem then is "trade diversion"--particularly for wheat and sugar, where the EC runs a chronic sur-plus--at the expense of Portugal's present major suppliers (United States, Argentina, Brazil). Will the Portuguese like to see the trading links estab-lished with these countries jeopardized? How will the displaced third-country suppliers react? An-other problem is increased competition from the Mediteranean countries as well as the ACP countries of the Lome Convention which are entitled, under the prevailing agreements, to sell commodities such

as fresh and processed fruit and vegetables, as well
as fish products to the Common Market totally or
partially exempted from customs duties and other
restrictions. Moreover, one should not overlook
the likelihood of an increased competitive pressure from Spain. Once Portugal's neighbor joins
the EC (presumably at the same time as Portugal
herself), trade barriers between the two Iberian
countries will have to be removed, thereby allowing
Spain's agricultural sector to reap the advantages
stemming from its considerable export potential
(especially in wine, olive oil, citrus fruit,
processed vegetables, rice, fish products); the
geographical proximity will favor the penetration
of the Portuguese market by reducing transport
costs.

For industry, the outlook is slightly different. With regard to the present Community the
overall trade effects might not be very large.
The 1972 preferential trade agreement has already
provided for substantial natural cuts of tariff
and non-tariff barriers, whereas rapid inflation
in Portugal has considerably reduced the incidence
of prevailing customs duties (since these are
specific rather than ad-valorem). This implies
that the adoption of the Common External Tariff
could even lead to increasing effective protection
of Portuguese manufacturers against imports from
the United States and Japan. Again, the major
source of competitive import expansion might be
the supply potential of Spain's industry, many
branches of which rank higher than the Portuguese
ones in terms of cost advantages, technological
superiority, and marketing expertise. Chemicals,
steel, machinery, ships, cars, electrical appliances are case in point. Furthermore, non-
European semi-industrial countries may also
accentuate their competitive pressure in Portuguese domestic market, once the country adopts the
EC's General System of Preferences, joins the Lome
Convention and adheres to the existing trade
agreements between the Community and a number of
Mediterranean countries (especially Israel). Labor
intensive industries such as clothing, textiles,
footwear, and travel goods are certainly those in
which production is endangered the most. On the
export side, Portuguese manufacturers will loose
the preferential treatment which they still enjoy
in the United States, Canada, Australia, New
Zealand, and Japan.

Turning to the second question--concerning the

effects on entry on growth--, I think that, on balance, these should be positive, provided appropriate policies are pursued. The agricultural sector, as backward as it is at present, has a potential for raising productivity levels. The adoptation of the EC's systems of price support and input subsidies might help improve the allocation of resources within this sector. And they might contribute to increase the incomes of Portuguese farmers and thereby their output (assuming that price-elasticity of the domestic supply is sufficiently positive at least in the medium run). There are eventually two factors running counter to this, however. One is that the Portuguese Escudo devalues with respect to the other European currencies, due to a relatively higher rate of inflation in Portugal. If this happens, the income of farmers will increase less as a result of the system of "monetary compensation amounts" (which would, however, benefit consumers). Second, the enlarged Community may continue to generate overproduction. In this case, budget constraints will inhibit that the prices paid to farmers remain as relatively favorable as they used to be.

Industrial growth could be stimulated through the impetus to factor productivity and investment. Most people would agree that wider markets facilitate the exploitation of economies of scale in given firms, that they open opportunities for introducing large-scale production in newly established plants, and that they permit increased specialization, both vertically and horizontally, on an optimum scale.

In addition, there is an efficiency aspect which receives, by comparison, much less attention, although it may turn out to be more important in practice. We know that in Portugal the prevailing levels of protection, regulations, and incentives have created considerable "X-inefficiency" at the firm level. Among the many high-cost producers there are not only those who would not be able to compete with imports but also those who could actually compete--if it was a matter of survival--by reducing costs. The latter firms are simply not on their production possibility frontiers, because their managers prefer a "quiet life" in spite of profit maximization, which is an attitude they can afford under protection and in view of the fact that domestic competition does not function sufficiently well in Portugal. Increased import competition from the EC and elsewhere might present a challenge to the ability of management of Portuguese firms to improve the organizational and technological efficiency, to intensify the control of quality, and even to develop and market new products. If this happens, Portuguese firms will appear as more competitive in their production for both export and import substitutes.

Improved "X-efficiency" and economies of scale might have a parallel effect on the volume of investment. New equipment will be needed in order to withstand foreign competition, to achieve specialization, and to increase the scale of production. Furthermore, complete new plants may be constructed in activities where Portugal's comparative advantage is particularly strong, reflecting also an inter-industry reallocation of resources, i.e., from lower- to higher-productivity and skill requirement sectors. At the same time, there will be disinvestment in the less efficient firms; whether or not this would cause the overall investment volume to fall or to only increase at modest rates, depends on the effectiveness with which government policies are pursued.

Apart from increased domestic savings, the inflow of foreign capital might remain an important source of financing a growing investment in Portugal. Braga de Macedo discusses foreign direct investment in terms of its balance of payments implications. There are three additional dimensions: First, Portugal could benefit in terms of a greater availability of equipment, know-how and entrepreneurship which it needs very badly. Second, incoming foreign investment could be a substitute for labor emigration from Portugal to the Northern part of the Community. Third, foreign firms could make an important contribution to bringing Portugal's industrial structure closer to the country's comparative advantages by strengthening both growth and diversification of manufactured exports.

Let us now consider the economic policy implications of what has been said so far. I know too little about Portugal's policy framework to give more than guidelines for designing sensible development policies. It seems to be important that the Portuguese Government (i) promote the modernization of the agricultural sector by rationalizing the systems of price support and input subsidies, improving credit facilities, undertaking and stimulating investments in irrigation and rural electrification, expanding extension services, and encouraging agricultural research;

(ii) complement trade liberalization policies with
adjustment assistance in favor of trade-impacted
workers, capital owners and regional budgets, but
avoid the provision of growth-inhibiting maintenance aids; manufactured exports should be promoted
at the same time, which might imply, inter alia,
the maintenance of the crawling-peg exchange rate
system; (iii) relax prevailing policies regulating
the sectoral and geographical allocation of
(private and public) manufacturing investments;
that it renounce permissive attitudes with regard
to restrictive business practices and strengthen
competition policies in order to allow the market
mechanism to direct resources to their most
efficient uses; but the Government should promote
at the same time mergers of firms where necessary
to achieve cost efficient sizes of plants; (iv)
allow state-owned companies or enterprises with
government participation to operate autonomously,
whereas the state should divest itself of its
ownership in such firms which do not require public
support for being commercially viable and concentrate, in turn, on activities involving a high
social rate of return on invested capital; (v) ease
prevailing job-tenure regulations which tend to
increase the real wage cost of labor (being in
large supply in Portugal) and to benefit only the
pool of labor actually employed; and allow the
structure of real wages to reflect the structure of
labor skills in order to avoid that qualified
labor, which is mobile, emigrates to the more
advanced countries; and (vi) reverse the strong
downward tendency in foreign direct investment
during the post-revolutionary years, by adequately
compensating expropriated foreigners and adhering
to clear and steady rules on these investments.

Some reforms in these directions have already
been initiated or are being designed. The crawling
peg and a new Foreign Investment Code (of August
1977) are cases in point. Given the risk of high
economic and political costs, too many policy
reversals cannot be brought about quickly. Hence,
there is a need for a gradual approach. This means
the announcement by the governments of a plan with
a sequence of policy reforms envisaged for several
years ahead, which is sensible and realistic and
may therefore influence positively the expectations of the private sector.

I end with a platitude which, however, under-
lines an important point: the Portuguese Government is facing the very difficult task to restore

private business confidence in the country's future
economic development. Only if it succeeds will
productive investment increase again, so that
overall growth can be accelerated and job opportunities rapidly expanded. Otherwise negotiations
with the EC might be lengthened considerably, since
the prevailing unemployment in the Community will
create much resistance against the possibility that
Portugal will export its own unemployment through
the enlarged common labor market. All this means
in the last analysis, that Portugal's entry into
the EC should not be considered as a panacea to
the many problems which the domestic economy is
suffering from at present. This is also the
message conveyed by Braga de Macedo.

Notes on the Contributors

SIMON SERFATY received his Ph.D. in Political Science from The Johns Hopkins University in 1967. A member of the faculty of The Johns Hopkins' School of Advanced International Studies in Washington, D.C. since 1972, he has served as Director of the School's Center of European Studies in Bologna, Italy (1972-76) and as Director of the School's Center of Foreign Policy Research (1977-80). His numerous publications include, most recently, Fading Partnership: America and Europe After 30 Years (1979).

JORGE BRAGA DE MACEDO received his Ph.D. in Economics from Yale University in 1979. A graduate of the University of Toulouse and of the Faculty in Law, University of Lisbon, he is now an Assistant Professor of Economics and International Affairs, and a faculty associate of the International Finance Section and the Research Program in Development Studies at Princeton University. Professor Braga de Macedo has worked in the Research Department of the International Monetary Fund, and he is a co-editor of Economia (Lisbon).

THOMAS C. BRUNEAU received his Ph.D. in Political Science from the University of California at Berkeley in 1970. A member of the faculty of Political Science at McGill University since 1969, Professor Bruneau has been the Director of the University's Center for Developing Area Studies since 1978. His many publications include, most recently, Os Portugueses e a Politica Quatro Anos Depois de 1974, with Mario Bacalhau (1978).

EUSEBIO MUJAL-LEON received his Ph.D. in Political Science from the Massachusetts Institute of Technology in 1979. He is now an Assistant Professor of Government at Georgetown University in Washington, D.C. He has written extensively on Iberian politics and his book entitled Communism and Political Change in Spain will be published next year.

JUAN J. LINZ is Pelatiah Perit Professor of Social and Political Science at Yale University. He is co-editor (with Alfred Stepan) of Crisis, Breakdown and Reequilibration, volume 1 of The Breakdown of Democratic Regimes (1978), and has contributed to books on authoritarian regimes, the sociology of fascism, national and local elites in Spain, and politics in Spain, Germany, Italy, and Brazil.

PAUL KRUGMAN is Associate Professor of Economics at the Massachusetts Institute of Technology, from which he obtained a Ph.D. in 1977. He previously taught at Yale. He has served as a consultant to the Banco de Portugal in 1976 and has written extensively on international trade and finance and macroeconomics of semi-industrialized economies.

SRIRAM AIYER received his Bachelor's degree in India, his Master's degree from Manchester University in the U.K., and obtained his Ph.D. from Cornell University in the U.S. He joined the World Bank in 1969 and has been Chief of Country Programs Division, dealing with Portugal and several countries in the Middle East, since 1976.

LUIS MIGUEL BELEZA is Associate Professor of Economics at the New University of Lisbon and a member of the research staff of the Banco de Portugal. He received a Ph.D. in Economics at the Massachusetts Institute of Technology in 1979 and taught previously at the Technical University of Lisbon and the Catholic University of Portugal. He has written several articles on international economics and macroeconomics of semi-industrialized economies.

BARBARA STALLINGS is an Assistant Professor of Political Science at the University of Wisconsin-Madison. Currently at work on a study dealing with

the role of the International Monetary Fund in
Europe, she has also written extensively on Latin
America, including "Peru and the U.S. Banks: The
Privatization of International Finance," in Richard
Fagen, ed., Capitalism and the State in U.S.-Latin
American Relations (1979).

PATRICK de FONTENAY received his Ph.D. in Economics
from Yale University in 1967.   After teaching at Vas-
sar he joined the staff of the International Bank
for Reconstruction and Development in 1965.   He
transferred to the staff of the International Monetary Fund in 1970, and has been a division chief in
the European Department there since 1973.

PENTTI J.K. KOURI is Professor of Economics at New
York University.   He was an economist in the Research Department of the International Monetary
Fund, obtained a Ph.D. in Economics at the Massachusetts Institute of Technology in 1975 and taught
previously at Stanford and Yale.   His many writings
include a model of growth in the small open economy
developed while he was a Visiting Scholar at the
University of Stockholm, which is published in Inflation and Unemployment in Small Open Economies,
A. Lindbeck, (ed).

HANS SCHMITT received his Ph.D. in Economics from
the University of California at Berkeley in 1959.
On the Economics faculty of the University of Wis-
consin until 1970, he first joined the staff of the
International Bank for Reconstruction and Development in 1965.   He transferred to the staff of the
International Monetary Fund in 1971 and has been a
division chief in the European Department there
since 1974.

JUERGEN B. DONGES is Professor of Economics at the
University of Kiel, Federal Republic of Germany, and
Director of the Department of Development Economics
at the Kiel Institute of World Economics.   He is a
noted expert on the Iberian economies and has written extensively on Spain and Portugal.